Faces of Diversity

Faces of Diversity

Nashá London-Vargas, Ph.D.

VANTAGE PRESS
New York

Copyright © 1999 by Nashá London-Vargas, Ph.D.

Published by Vantage Press, Inc.
516 West 34th Street, New York, New York 10001

Manufactured in the United States of America
ISBN: 0-533-12777-7

Library of Congress Catalog Card No.: 98-90375

0 9 8 7 6 5 4 3 2 1

God hath given you one face and you make yourselves another.
—W. Shakespeare

I give thanks to my Heavenly Father for giving me the faith, hope, strength, and the confidence to grow and progressively move forward in my life.

To my husband Salvador, who has been a true friend and companion throughout this adventure, you have been someone I can talk to about all which concerns me, and have somehow managed to make me feel good about myself no matter what the circumstances have been. You are definitely a breath of fresh air and a ray of sunshine in my life. I thank you and B.B. (Bootie Bird) for your unconditional love and support.

To my mother Kersena, brother Lesean, and sister Khaleah, you three have been the perfect canvas in my life. From our shared experiences, I have been given the courage to embrace change and to trust life. I thank you for allowing me the opportunity to be myself when I needed to the most and for staying close by offering your love and support. I am here in this space and time because of my family.

Contents

List of Tables

Faces of Diversity

Part One

A Scenario-Based Study of Black and White Workers' Perception of Leaders' Desirability as Leaders and Leaders' Diversity Acceptance: An Application of Thomas' Three Levels of Diversity Implementation

Racism within corporate America has affected work relationships among White and Black workers (Yamato, 1992). Although racism appears to be simple in its structure (perceived attitudes and feelings), it is difficult to eliminate due to the power and privilege granted to one race group over another (Yamato, 1992). Yamato further suggests White workers are the beneficiaries of institutional racism in America; hence, they are in a position to not care about the issues and concerns of Black workers within the workplace. With such a distinction between power and privilege among White and Black workers, Black workers are usually more aware of the ill effects of White racism within the workplace because the injustices within the institution have an immediate impact on their situation (Alderfer, 1982; Bonacich, 1992; Henderson, 1994). Individual and group experience of and responses to race, power, and privilege are formed through ethnic identity development (Rotheram, 1987, Phinney, 1987).

Higher ethnic identity awareness has been shown to correlate with greater acceptance of diversity (Phinney, 1992). With the understanding that White and Black workers enter the workforce with different levels of ethnic identity awareness, we would expect them to show differences in

1

their attitudes toward both leaders' acceptance of diversity and diversity efforts at work.

Several types of diversity acceptance and implementation have been categorized by Thomas (1991, 1996). Thomas argues that, in addition to utilizing programs such as Affirmative Action and valuing differences, managers within corporate America should take measures to increase interactions among their diverse workforce, specifically White and Black workers (Thomas, 1991). He believes managers should identify special needs of the workers, and be flexible enough to work through episodes of conflict. Thomas posits three levels of diversity implementation:

- Affirmative Action
- valuing differences
- managing diversity

Based on Thomas' three categories, this research supports the belief that Black and White workers desire to work for leaders whose style of managing diversity is more all-inclusive than leaders who manage diversity issues within the workplace through measures of Affirmative Action or valuing differences. This research also offers mixed support. Ethnic identity development (EID) and ethnicity, when looked at together, do affect how Black and White workers perceive diversity acceptance and how desirable their leaders are to work for.

Chapter I
Introduction

The purpose of this study is to explore the ethnic identity development of White and Black workers and its affects on perceived leader acceptance of diversity and the desirability of working for a White or Black leader. This research is exploratory in the sense that the literature on Black and White work race relations and their perceptions of diversity is quite limited. Much of the literature written about race relations in America focuses primarily on Whites and Minorities; thus, the literature reviewed to support the assumptions in this study will be drawn from Minority literature.

The significance of this study is to provide a better understanding of what White and Black workers perceive to be diversity and how the various issues of diversity should be addressed by either a White or Black leader. Such knowledge can provide further insight into improving work race relations between White and Black workers/leaders and aid White and Black leaders in their task of examining the effectiveness of their leadership style in managing diversity within the workplace. In addition, this research will serve as a test of Thomas' categories of diversity. Thomas asserts that the category of "diversity management" is the most inclusive and important of his specified approaches (Affirmative Action, valuing differences, and diversity management). This research will help determine if leaders identified with each approach are perceived as having different levels of diversity acceptance.

Definitions

Black

Throughout this study the racial label of "Black" will be used instead of "African-American." Although the racial label African-American may be politically correct in today's American society, it does not correctly identify the ethnic origin of all Blacks living in America, and is limited in its expression of a rich history that illustrates the past and present race relations of Black and White Americans. Thus, the ethnic label Black is universal in its application and appropriately describes the "Black" experience in America.

White

Throughout this study the racial label of "White" will be used to refer to people of the Caucasian racial heritage. It should be noted that in the United States "Whites" are sometimes referred to as Anglo-Americans or as Euro-Americans. Since both of these terms refer to specific sub-groups of Caucasians, the more inclusive term "White" is used in this study.

Ethnic Identity

Ethnic identity is defined as an individual's ability to identify with an ethnic group as a member (sense of belonging), with a level of awareness of self and others as ethnic group members (ethnic identity achievement), and with a display of ethnic behaviors that are specific to their group (Phinney, 1992).

Diversity

Diversity is defined as a leaders' choice in implementing strategies based on Affirmative Action, valuing differences, or diversity management in an attempt to meet the diverse needs of its White and Black workers (Thomas, 1991).

The Developmental Processes of Ethnic Identity

The ethnic identity development and ethnic socialization processes differ among White and Black Americans in that each ethnic group possesses experiences, attitudes, beliefs, feelings, and behavioral patterns which help define the individual and group members' ethnicity in relation to other ethnic groups (Phinney, 1992). Such developmental differences influence our perceptions of how we view the world. As adults, White and Black workers bring to their work environment their experiences and perceptions as ethnic group members, which helps them define what is relevant to their diverse group and individual experiences and how they believe such issues should be addressed, by their leader(s). While White and Black workers bring with them their own definitions of what diversity is and how issues of diversity should be addressed, White and Black leaders have also defined what diversity means in the workplace and have adopted leadership styles to resolve issues surrounding diversity. Most often the many definitions possessed by both workers and leaders do not coincide, which makes it difficult to manage diversity and improve race relations among workers and workers/leaders (Thomas, 1991). With Workforce 2000 steadily growing in diversity, corporate leaders will need to become more flexible in how they view and address diversity if they are to create a work environment that allows each worker to perform at an optimal level.

For the past ten years, corporate America has been preparing itself for the major demographic changes that are to occur by the year 2000. Based on statistical data, it is being predicted that Workforce 2000 will consist primarily of Minorities, women, older age groups, immigrants, and an increasing gap between workers with advanced education and those workers who can barely read or write. Workforce 2000 will greatly differ from the workforce of the past in that until recently White males made up the dominant work group and Blacks and Latinos were the visible Minority ethnic groups (Jamieson and O'Mara, 1991). According to Jamieson and O'Mara (1991), the future workforce will be reflective of many cultural groups. The workforce will reflect a wide variety of Asian cultures and a mixture

5

of Middle Eastern and Arab cultures (Jamieson and O'Mara, 1991). The White majority work group is becoming a "Minority" in many organizations. People of color who are born in the United States and immigrant minorities are expected to comprise forty-three percent of new entrants to the workforce by the year 2000 (Jamieson and O'Mara, 1991).

This proliferation of cultural backgrounds within the workplace brings to the surface a variety of values, work ethics, and norms of behavior toward diversity, which are ethnically and culturally rooted (Jamieson and O'Mara, 1991). The concept "diversity" carries with it a variety of organizational definitions as well. How an organization chooses to define "diversity" will determine how issues of diversity are managed. This, in turn, will impact effectiveness of work relationships between managers and workers. Thus, the present study will explore the differences in perceptions of White and Black leaders' acceptance of diversity and how desirable to work for the leader is among White and Black workers.

Thomas (1991) refers to diversity as a collective of all differences and similarities, including culture, ethnicity, race, socioeconomic background, gender, sexual orientation, age, physical abilities, languages, religious beliefs, education, and lifestyles. Thomas (1991) further defines Affirmative Action as a legal initiative which seeks to prevent discrimination because of race, gender, age, disability, religion, or national origin.

During the ten years that corporate America has been attempting to manage its diverse workforce population, workers have been involved in a barrage of programs and workshops that are designed to explain the objectives of Affirmative Action and valuing differences. Affirmative Action programs in organizations focus on providing equal opportunities within the structure for women and Minority workers (Thomas, 1991). Valuing-differences workshops are designed to increase awareness about similarities and differences and to decrease undesirable behavior among employees (Thomas, 1991).

Although well-intended, these programs fall short of their goals in improving race relations among employees. They occur over brief periods of time and thus have only limited impact (Thomas, 1991). Further, Yamato argues that such programs do not directly address the real issues of race, and only indirectly address racism through agendas such as "sexism," heteroism, and physicalism (Yamato, 1992). Thomas contends that Affirmative Action and valuing-differences programs are not sufficient; however, such programs should not be dismissed. Instead they should be coupled with a more current approach, "diversity management."

According to Thomas, diversity management is a process in which managers create a work environment which allows workers to make their fullest contributions (Thomas, 1991). For Thomas, the fundamental differences between the three approaches (Affirmative Action, valuing differences, and managing diversity) are based on legal and moral issues. While Affirmative Action is a legal mandate and valuing differences is an educational process of recognition and acceptance of diversity, diversity management is more expansive. Diversity management is the process of creating a work environment that is supportive of employee differences and similarities. Diversity management is a business strategy that is designed to help organizations remain competitive in a changing market place and equip organizations with the necessary tools needed to retain existing talent and attract new talent. The objective of diversity management is to create a work environment that allows each individual worker to bring into the workplace their values, beliefs, culture, enabling them to perform at an optimal level without any restraints on their character.

Thomas (1991) contends that managers who attempt to manage diversity should ask themselves the following questions about manager and employee work relations:

1. "Why doesn't the system work naturally for everyone?"
2. "What has to be done to allow it to do so?"
3. "Will the cultural roots of this company allow us to take the necessary corrective action?"
4. "If not, what root changes do we have to make?"

Thomas (1994) suggests that in addition to changing those elements which hold in place and allow for discriminatory employment practices (Affirmative Action), corporate America will need to shift its focus from Eurocentric ways of managing its women and Minority workers. In addition, organizations must become more flexible in learning about the cultural experiences of all employees (Thomas, 1994). Thomas argues that corporate America has managed to convince its workers that corporate success is "color-blind," "gender-blind," and "lifestyle-blind." However, if corporate America is really serious about tapping into the full potential of all of its human resources, then it must come to the realization of color, gender, and lifestyle differences. Corporate America must realize that America is a capitalistic, racially divided country where one's differences and similarities with respect to race do matter (Bonacich, 1992).

According to Henderson (1994), any attempt to examine race differences within the workplace needs to begin with exploration in the following three areas:

1. Institutional structures and personal behavior, and the relationship between the two
2. The variation in both degree and form of expression of individual prejudice
3. The fact that racism is but one form of a larger and more inclusive pattern of ethnocentrism that may be based on a number of factors, many of which are nonracial in character

The exploration of institutional racism and its affect on interracial relations among White and Black workers and the varying degrees of individual prejudice is best illustrated in a study conducted by Block, Roberson, and Neuger (1992). Based on their study, Block, Roberson, and Neuger suggest that most of the policy and decision makers in corporate America are White; therefore, it is important to explore their attitudes toward the general goals around workforce diversity and the treatment of different races. It is also important to examine their perceptions of how individuals from different races are treated within the workplace, their beliefs about what measures should be taken to resolve issues of diversity, and how to become involved in diversity issues within the workplace (Block, Roberson, and Neuger, 1992). Thus, not only should workplaces become inclusive but so should policy and decision making become inclusive, of multiple cultures. However, inclusion may be more difficult than simply having Blacks present in organizational processes.

Many Black workers of Workforce 2000 believe that not much has changed in the way of on-the- job discrimination. According to Blauner (1992), Black workers believe that institutionalized racism, in all its subtlety, is the main obstacle that prevents them from moving up the corporate ladder and interferes with interpersonal communication with Whites. They contend that the trouble with race relations in America is that American culture is rooted in capitalism and division among the races. Within the corporate setting, this drive for power and privilege between the races keeps managers and workers focused on racism, which makes it difficult to resolve issues that pertain to diversity within the organization (Steele, 1990).

According to Steele, the race struggle in America has always been one of power and privilege for Whites. The history that exists between Black Americans and White Americans has always been Whites believing that they are entitled to power and privilege, therefore entitled to subjugate Blacks (Steele, 1990). West (1993) suggests that the accumulated effects of White racism that Blacks have suffered has created wounds and scars, which are deeply seated in anger, a boiling sense of rage, and a passionate pessimistic view toward America's will to justice. Thus, Black and White Americans continue to experience American society in very different ways (Wilkins, 1996). Whites experience a sense of ownership and belonging in America as they are entitled to accomplish and advance throughout their lives (education, career, healthcare, housing) without interference from Black discrimination (Wilkins, 1996). On the other hand, Blacks experience tremendous hardship as they seek to obtain some sense of ownership and belongingness in American society (Wilkins, 1996). This is due in part to the very existence of Blacks in America being challenged and confronted by White discrimination (Wilkins, 1996).

This argument may shed light on the fact that there continues to be an overrepresentation of Blacks at the bottom of American organizations (entry level positions), while there is an overrepresentation of Whites at the top of American organizations (executives, managers, supervisors) (Bonacich, 1992). Due to this lop-sided distribution of power and privilege within corporate America, it is commonplace to have Black workers complain about the ill-treatment they experience on a daily basis while working for their White leaders (Bonacich, 1992). Also, to the contrary, it is not unusual for White workers to be numb to their fellow Black workers' plight because they are not directly experiencing White racism within the corporation (Henderson, 1994). This could lead to very different perceptions by Black and White workers of diversity acceptance. Thus, exploring workers' perceptions of leaders' diversity acceptance is important to resolving issues of diversity that may lead to inter-group conflict and, with this awareness, the possibility of improving employee work relations may become more of a reality. In efforts to better understand the ethnic identity development of White and Black workers, managers will be able to better identify those elements within an organization that contribute to negative group perceptions of "self" and others, all of which makes it difficult for managers to manage workers and their work.

Although many aspects of White and Black history within America may be viewed as tragic and devastating, the notion of moving forward toward a better understanding of one another as individuals and as ethnic group members must begin with becoming fully enlightened of the ethnic socialization processes of both White and Black Americans and how each racial group's interpretation of diversity approaches influence day-to-day activities inside organizations.

Chapter II
Review of the Literature

Race and Oppression: Effects on Perception Differences

White and Black workers bring to the workplace a history of racial division. Berg (1984) argues that this history precedes every facet of American life. White Americans are familiar with their place of power and privilege and Black Americans are familiar with their societal position of having less power and privilege than Whites. However, most of the interactions occur at the unconscious level, and often groups are not aware of how their group membership affects interpretation of the behavior of other racial group members (Berg, 1984). Thus, Whites and Blacks have had a difficult time working together (Berg, 1984).

The interpersonal dynamics within an organization are much too complex to funnel into a single dimension or origin. This is particularly true of the interpersonal relations that exist between White and Black workers. Whites and Blacks hold a unique position within America's past as well as its history. Historically, Blacks are the only race group whose entrance into America began with slavery (Alderfer, 1982). Blacks have been held in an inferior position to Whites through mass media, politics, and institutional advancement for over three hundred years (Alderfer, 1982).

Alderfer suggests that the concept of racism is useful to understand not only the three-hundred-year race relationship between Whites and Blacks in the United States, but also the current-day race relationship. Despite the progressive changes that have occurred over the past twenty years, Whites remain the dominant group in America, therefore having more opportunities to demonstrate racism than Blacks (Alderfer, 1982). America's historical evidence indicates that White people with power have had a tendency to dominate Blacks through various elements of "racism" (Aldefer, 1982). Through the racial exploitation of Blacks, Whites

11

were able to build this nation (the United States sanctioned slavery while the colonial economy benefited from the slave economy) (Alderfer, 1982). This view of White racism has led to the belief that "the United States is a racist society that is capitalist and racially divided to promote its gains" (Henderson, 1994).

Present-day race relations among Blacks and Whites has not changed much. Whites are still in the position of power and privilege and Blacks continue to hold on to their position of less power and privilege (McIntosh, 1988). Many Whites and Blacks have managed to look beyond their past familial ties as slave owners and slaves and individually manage the differences between them in hopes of a more productive life. This must also be accomplished by the work system (corporate America), which needs to release its ties to racism and oppression if all workers (Black *and* White) are to move on with the business of obtaining a better quality of work life (improved race relations, increased productivity, and job satisfaction) (Berg, 1984).

The Multi-Levels of White racism

According to Wilson (1973), White racism occurs at five levels:

- cultural
- biological
- institutional
- collective
- individual

First, at the cultural level, we can examine the initial contact Whites had with Blacks in America, which established race relations. Black and White American history is unique in that it is the only race relation in which one group of people felt it necessary to enslave the other because Blacks were believed to be culturally inferior (Wilson, 1973). Through cultural racism, Whites have discriminated against Blacks because of such cultural differences as language, lifestyle, religion, customs, rituals, and dress (Wilson, 1973).

Second, given that Blacks have physical characteristics that are different from Whites', this has also been grounds for White Americans to oppress Blacks and to justify American Black slavery (Wilson, 1973).

12

There have been numerous studies done (scientific and nonscientific) to examine these differences and to explain how Blacks are believed to be both mentally and biologically inferior to Whites. Such studies have lost their scientific and nonscientific strength through the years as rebuttal studies have been conducted to expose the White cultural bias in the data (Banton, 1987). However, the image of Blacks being unsophisticated people has left a lasting impression within American culture among Blacks, Whites, and other ethnic groups (Banton, 1987).

Third, institutional racism is the form of White racism that strangles the upward mobility and progression of the Black racial group and justifies the high status of Whites in America. The dominant culture in America is White culture. More Whites than Blacks, make the laws, run both formal and informal learning institutions, and regulate housing. Whites believe that Blacks cannot make conscientious decisions to run a country, are too inferior intellectually to compete with Whites, and are too unsavory to live with. Black Americans have and continue to remain underrepresented in all three categories (Banton, 1987).

Fourth, through collective racism, Whites have managed to deny Blacks their full rights as American citizens by establishing their beliefs about Blacks as truth and passing the beliefs on to the next generation reinforcing White ideology on a daily basis (Banton, 1987). The power and privileges that Whites are entitled to in America goes without question and excludes Blacks (McIntoch, 1988).

Fifth, White racism is also visible at the individual level. White individuals, whether they are conscious or unconscious about the power and privilege they have inherited from their forefathers at the expense of exploiting Blacks, are influenced by White racism by way of their White group membership. Being in such an empowered and privileged position, Whites have not been placed in an inferior position where they are confronted with who they are and how they fit in American society as Blacks must do on a daily basis.

McIntosh (1988) contends that White privilege is a condition which effects the daily lives of Whites and establishes their social identity among themselves and with other ethnic groups. Through their status of power and privilege, Whites can be assured higher education, preferred housing, career opportunities, and a life not affected by racism nor discrimination (McIntosh, 1988). In her extensive write-up on White privilege, McIntosh lists forty-six conditions of daily experiences which benefit Whites. Among those conditions are the following privileges of Whites in the U.S.:

13

- They can avoid spending time with Blacks
- They are guaranteed to live in any area they can afford and/or want
- They are guaranteed to see positive images of themselves in the media
- They are taught that their race group made American History what it is
- They are guaranteed educational rights without facing discrimination
- They are allowed to ignore the plight of people of color

This privilege held by many Whites makes it difficult to become aware of who they are as White people and how their Whiteness affects people of color, specifically Blacks (Alderfer, 1982). Alderfer contends that Whites do not have to define themselves in terms of race; hence, they continue to have difficulty working with and managing the cultural differences that Blacks possess. Within corporate America, Blacks are still finding themselves as an underrepresented group and are faced with the ills of White racism in their work relations with Whites (Alderfer, 1982).

Prejudice in America

According to Berg (1984), "The concept of prejudice includes at least three basic elements: a) negative attitudes, b) a yard stick, point of reference, or factual base from which to evaluate these attitudes and judgments, and c) the necessary precondition of existing relationships between groups."

1. Negative attitudes derive from the need to sanction feelings of conflict and hostility that emerge during times of competition and survival.
2. Negative attitudes within a group must be displaced onto another group in order to sustain group cohesiveness for the purpose of group survival and productivity.
3. Groups and individuals compare themselves socially and this process of social comparison is the basis of group identity. This group identity forms the necessary bonds for group members to meet their needs.

The values and beliefs individuals learn as group members and the tensions and frustrations that groups experience while competing for scarce resources against another culturally different group is a root cause of ethnic prejudices (Henderson, 1994). In an effort to see how ethnic prejudices are intertwined into the fabric of American society and how all citizens are affected by its ill-effects, its by-products "racism and stereotyping" must be addressed (Henderson, 1984).

White racism in America is the act of stereotyping or the formation of invalid ethnic notions. According to Allport (1979), stereotyping usually plays a role in interracial interactions when anxiety coupled with ambiguity increase and "people tend to define their deteriorated situations in terms of scapegoats." Hence, stereotyping is also instrumental in keeping racial groups divided. The White American stereotypes that have been portrayed about Minorities, especially Blacks, are constantly fed to the world through highly influential mass media on a daily basis. For example, Blacks are portrayed as lazy, unintelligent, sexual, and aggressive (Allport, 1979).

Another element of White racism in America is the promoted ideology that Blacks are culturally, physically, biologically, and socially different than Whites. This perceived difference between the groups has entitled Whites to be more superior than Blacks (Alderfer, 1982). For example:

1. Vogt's typology theory suggests that the intellectual development of Blacks peaks at adolescence, and that Blacks in America have smaller brains than Blacks in Africa, which explains why Black American slaves had to be treated badly.
2. Parks social ecology theory implies that Blacks are naturally inferior to Whites and, as they did during slavery, Blacks will accept their inferior position to Whites and form friendly relations with Whites (Banton, 1987). These beliefs have made it possible for White racism to "demean, subvert, destroy the present condition or future potential of members of the Black racial group" (Alderfer, 1982).

Due to the status of power and privilege that Whites hold in America, they have been afforded the opportunity of being overly exposed to the "undesirable" behavior of Blacks, more so than Blacks are exposed to the "undesirable" behaviors of Whites (Tajfel, 1982). Given that Whites in the

15

U.S. have dealt with people of color almost exclusively on a level of Whites being superior in power and knowledge, it has become a natural tendency for Whites to stereotype Blacks as an inferior race (Bender, and Leone, 1996). Whites have found themselves in the forefront of corporate group discussions and workshops in dealing with workforce diversity. Through corporate programs and workshops, such as diversity training and valuing differences, White participants have found and continue to find themselves in the position of "the oppressor."

Whites in general do not see themselves as "the oppressor" even if they assign this label to their forefathers. When given such a label by Blacks within these workshops Whites usually become defensive (Kuran, 1996). They take the stand of reverse discrimination also referred to as White backlash (Kuran, 1996). Kuran suggests that "since the Civil Rights victories of the 1960s, a recurring theme in American politics has been one of an unfolding 'White backlash' against policies designed to benefit Blacks." Individual Whites may take the initiative to examine who they are as a White person and how their Whiteness may have a negative effect in their interactions with Blacks in the workplace. Ethnic notions which derive from negative stereotyping have a tremendous amount of influence in how we perceive ourselves and others and how we are perceived by others.

This view of White racism has led to the belief that "race" is at the core of categorizing ideas about human differences in America (Allport, 1979). Based on the above examples, it is quite clear that the elements of prejudice (racism and stereotyping) play important roles in how group memberships and group identities are formed. Steele (1990) contends that racial group membership influences our perception and interpretation of other group members and events, and these perceptions and interpretations produce the data that shapes our beliefs about ourselves and others. Thus, the present research will explore the effects of racial group membership on perceived leader diversity acceptance and desirability to work for these leaders among White and Black workers.

Class Prejudice

Thus far the focus has been on White racism, privilege, and prejudice. These are so interrelated that the influences of each would be difficult to pinpoint (Blauner, 1992). Though these variables do directly affect workplace interactions, an additional social variable (class) must be considered to give a more complete picture. Class prejudice effects economic distribution (Blauner, 1992). This in turn partially determines distribution of Blacks and Whites in the workplace hierarchy. After examining the effects of class prejudice on interracial relations within the workplace, we will consider how management may deal with assimilation of Blacks into this economic stratification.

The economic situation in America is bewildering when one looks at the portion of those who have and those who have not. Blauner (1992) argues that America's philosophy of capitalism "by any means necessary" has divided its racial groups in several ways with respect to class (upper class, middle class, and lower class):

- gender and class status
- race and class status
- gender, race, and class status.

This could imply that the variables of White racism and oppression (discussed earlier in this study) are interrelated with economic issues of class.

Bell (1996) contends that economic statistics show that Blacks as a group fall far behind Whites in income and other measures of wealth. According to Bonacich (1992) and Bell (1996), class prejudice among the races is most obvious in comparisons between the economic power of Whites and the lack of economic power held by Blacks. Blacks are twice as likely to be unemployed than Whites, and three times more likely to live below the poverty level (Bell, 1996). And, within corporate America, Blacks are overrepresented in low-paying job categories, while Whites are overrepresented in high-paying job categories (Bonacich, 1992; Bell, 1996). Hacker (1996) contends that today, "Blacks remain underrepresented in the professions of engineering, law, medicine, architecture, and journalism." Blacks are also overrepresented in the professions of data entry, security guards, cab drivers, hotel maids, nursing aides, and postal clerks (Hacker, 1996).

Bonacich (1992) suggests that this portrait of America's class prejudice system is reflective of a capitalistic society that depends on the imbalance of power and wealth (privilege) to sustain itself. Thus, the careers and lives of Blacks, due to their skin color, will continue to be threatened by White discrimination in America (Bell, 1996).

17

Race and Diversity at Work

Griggs and Louw (1994) contend that White racism within organization life usually goes unaddressed because Whites have a difficult time in distinguishing the conscious and unconscious forms of racism in which they indulge. For example, television programs almost always portray Black Americans as criminals and janitors. Meanwhile, Whites are usually portrayed as judges and police (Griggs, and Louw, 1994). Within organizations, similar forms of conscious racism is permitted as long as Whites are shown in a favorable light and Blacks in a less favorable light. For example, it is common to hear humorous jokes about Blacks, but not about Whites (Alderfer, 1982). This form of unconscious racism has molded the posture of workplace assimilation (Thomas, 1991). Within the workplace, White workers are at liberty to bring their values and beliefs into the establishment (Thomas, 1991). However, Blacks are expected to leave their cultural identity "at the door" and take on the values of the White majority if they wish to survive the environment and compete on the White man's terms (Bonacich, 1992).

In addition to being denied career opportunities and experiencing racial tension at work, Black workers are also expected to work in a White environment where skin color is nonexistent (Bonacich, 1992). The various forms of conscious and unconscious White racism continues to drive a wedge between work relationships among White and Black workers (Bromely, and Longino, Jr., 1978). If there is to be any hope of creating a work environment that values all its workers, the issues of racism must be exposed and addressed (Thomas, 1991).

Ethnic Identity Development During Childhood

The negative attitudes adult workers bring to the workplace about their ethnic group status is rooted in perceptions conceived during childhood. In an effort to better understand the factors that influence and motivate tension among White and Black workers, it is necessary to examine research which focuses on the ethnic identity development of children (Rotheram and Phinney, 1987; Williams and Morland, 1976).

According to Rotheram and Phinney (1987), our ethnic identity is a compilation of awareness of self and others, feelings about self and others, and behavioral patterns that are specific to an ethnic group. Based on a number of developmental models of ethnic identity, Rotheram and Phinney contend that children go through several stages of ethnic awareness beginning at the age of three to age ten. Between the ages of three and four children become aware of color differences, emerging racial attitudes, and awareness of ethnic groups by social comparison. At ages four to eight, children begin to make strong preferences for one ethnic group or another for various reasons, and they are aware of ethnic group affiliations. And, between the ages of eight to ten children's attitudes toward their ethnicity and that of others begin to crystallize, and they become more curious about other ethnic groups. Although developmental models, which illustrate the progression of ethnic and racial awareness, vary slightly in the exact age such processes actually occur, they assist us in analyzing the ethnic socialization of children, specifically White and Black children, and how this process effects their perceptions and attitudes of self and others as ethnic group members.

In efforts to assess ethnic self-identification, ethnic attitudes, and stereotypes and prejudice toward others, Rotheram and Phinney (1987) offer several measurements:

1. Self-identification in young children can be assessed by presenting them with a series of pictures and dolls representing various ethnic groups. The objective is to have children select the object that is most like themselves.
2. Ethnic attitudes can be assessed by using a continuous rating scale to measure a child's preference for an ethnic group.
3. Stereotypes and prejudices can be assessed by evaluating how children rate their preference for an ethnic group over another on a continuous rating scale. Children that are more secure in their own self-identity are more likely to have a less negative attitude than those children who are less secure in their self-identity.

The Effects of Race and Color

With all of the importance placed on race, American children are introduced to the dynamics of race and color at a very early age (Williams, and Morland, 1976). Such early associations become embedded within cultural dimensions such as language. Williams and Morland contend that children make distinctions about race based on the English language use of color. As American history illustrates, White Americans have placed importance on skin to draw a line between superiority and inferiority among the races. Williams and Morland contend that these relationships could only have been established through language. In contemporary language, the colors "white" and "black" carry a variety of meanings. In our everyday speech we use the colors white and black to convey negative and positive expressions. The following examples of the color black are not exclusive nor inclusive with respect to the American culture (Williams, and Morland, 1979):

1. Black—a color that is opposite of white; black is dark, sad, evil, and not pure
2. Blacklist—to avoid an undesirable person
3. Black sheep—a dissolute family member
4. Blackmail—the act of extortion of money by threat
5. Blackguard—a villain
6. Black magic—witchcraft
7. Blackball—is a negative vote or exclusion
8. Black market—illegal trade
9. Black-hearted—a wicked person
10. Black reputation—a ruined reputation

Although there are some positive meanings associated with the color black, such as black pearl, the daily use of the color black to express negative connotations makes it difficult to think of the positive meanings. On the other hand, the American language use of the color white is associated with positive connotations. The following usages of the color white are not exclusive nor inclusive with respect to the American culture (Williams, and Morland, 1976):

1. White—the color opposite of black; it is pure and clean
2. White-collar—a professional employee
3. White hope—a promising person
4. White lie—a harmless fib/lie
5. Whitewash—to conceal errors

Generally speaking, white is used to express all that is good and black is used to express all that is bad in American culture (Williams and Morland, 1976). Given that language is essential in our existence, attitudes and ideas about color that are conveyed by parents, teachers, playmates, and mass media strongly influence how children and later adults learn to interpret the world (Williams, and Morland, 1976).

According to Williams and Morland, there are two ways in which color relates to race:

· skin color
· our natural ability as humans to be conscientious of color

Within America racial groups are not classified by their heritage and or cultural backgrounds, but are classified by colors (Williams and Morland, 1976). Euro-Americans are classified as white, African-Americans are classified as black, Asian-Americans are classified as yellow, and American-Indians are classified as red. Interesting enough these color codes for racial groups are not true representatives of the race groups themselves. Still, these labels have more of an influence on how we perceive and treat one another than by using the appropriate labels of ethnicity (Williams and Morland, 1976).

To further examine how one's skin color influences how we feel about ourselves and others, Williams and Morland conducted a study on racial preference. Within their study, Williams, and Morland (1976) had White and Black junior high and high school students rate their attitudes toward a variety of race and color concepts on a semantic differential scale. Among the concepts rated were "White American," and "Black American" (Williams and Morland, 1976). They used Evaluation (E) Scores where low E scores indicated a favorable attitude and high E scores indicated a less favorable attitude. Williams and Morland (1976) found the following: White sixth-grade students rated "White American" more favorably than "Black American." This trend was consistent throughout junior high and high school years. Black sixth grade students also rated "White Americans" more favorably than "Black Americans." However, Black eighth, tenth, and twelfth graders rated "Black Americans" more favorably than "White Americans." Williams and Morland suggested that the variation in scores among the Black students may have been reflective of the process of racial identity development.

As indicated by the above studies, Black children, unlike White children, go through a series of ethnic identity developmental stages by the time they reach high school. Based on their socially "inferior" status to Whites, Blacks are forced to recognize and examine their ethnicity and how it affects racial relationships within and outside of their ethnic group.

Ethnic Identity and Its Effects on Perception Differences

America is a racially divided country, and depending on where a particular racial group falls a certain amount of power and privilege is or is not experienced by the racial group. According to Block, Roberson, and Neuger, the racial development that is forced upon each and every American is a natural process. Our racial identity is instrumental in how we perceive ourselves as well as other racial group members. Ethnic identity also influences how we feel toward one another (Block, Roberson, and Neuger, 1992). The ethnic identity development of Black Americans began probably at the onset of White American slavery, with such questions as "Why have we as a people been chosen to endure and experience such an inhumane way of living?" and "Where and how do we as a people fit into White American culture?" (West, 1994). Although these questions still plague the Black community and the questions still go unanswered, Blacks have had to define themselves in relation to their inferior status to White Americans (West, 1994). Through this inferior status Blacks have been denied adequate healthcare, housing, education, and equal representation within Corporate America, beyond entry-level positions. Through the following passage, Henderson gives an example of Black ethnic identity development:

Black children begin life facing higher survival odds than White children. They are more likely to die in infancy than White babies. If a Black baby lives, the chances of losing his or her mother in childbirth is four times as high as the White baby. The baby is usually born into a family that lives in the inner city (over 75 percent of the 30 million African-American population does). The Black baby is usually born into a much larger family than the White baby and is forced to live in crowed housing. The Black family is forced to exist on a median family income that is barely half the median of White family income. Black adolescents are raised in an environment that sees less fame and fortune as opposed to White adolescents. And they are taught in schools that have inferior equipment and facilities. The education gap between Black and White employees of the same age often approaches two to three years (Henderson, 1994).

The "ethnic socialization" process White and Black American children experience leads them to internalize the behavioral patterns, attitudes, values, and perceptions of an ethnic group and to further make distinctions of themselves and others belonging to a particular ethnic group (Rotheram and Phinney, 1987). For children, there is a certain amount of ethnic identity awareness that accompanies age. Research that has focused on the ethnic identity development of adolescents and adults indicate that an individual's ethnic identity becomes more "consolidated" with age (Phinney, 1992).

Ethnic Identity Development of Black Americans and Their Perceptions of Self and Others

Phinney's three-stage Ethnic Identity Model for adolescents examines three aspects of ethnic identity that are universal among Black and Minority adolescents:

- unexamined ethnic identity
- ethnic identity search
- achieved ethnic identity

The first stage, unexamined ethnic identity, is characterized by an individual's lack of concern with ethnicity. This stage does not question the values and preferences of White America (Phinney, 1993). Unexamined ethnic identity is based on Cross's model of Black ethnic identity (pre-encounter) (Phinney, 1993). The second stage, ethnic identity search, focuses on an individual's ability to seek meaning in their ethnicity (Phinney, 1973). This stage is reflective of stages two and three (encounter and immersion/emersion) of Cross's Black ethnic identity model (Phinney, 1993). The final stage, achieved ethnic identity, identifies an individual as having a clear sense of ethnicity and is confident in making decisions based on their ethnicity (Phinney, 1973). This stage is also similar to Cross's fourth stage (internalization) (Phinney, 1993). In addition to examining the stages of ethnic identity development (unexamined ethnic identity, ethnic identity search, and achieved ethnic identity), Phinney created a measure which would allow further exploration of elements of ethnic identity that are common across ethnic groups (Multigroup Ethnic Identity Measure, or MEIM) (Phinney, 1992).

The MEIM measure explores the elements of self-identification, a sense of belonging, and attitudes toward one's group, which are common within the ethnic identity development of all ethnic groups (Phinney, 1992). Phinney contends that self-identification differs from ethnic identity and ethnicity, it allows an individual to make distinctions between parental background and sociological labels (Phinney, 1992).

The MEIM has three sub-scales:

- positive ethnic attitudes and sense of belonging
- ethnic identity achievement
- ethnic behaviors or practices

The design of the MEIM consists of fourteen items which represent positive ethnic attitudes and sense of belonging (five items); ethnic identity achievement/exploration and resolution of identity issues (seven items); and behaviors or practices (two items) (Phinney, 1992). Individuals rated the items by using a four-point scale from "strongly agree" to "strongly disagree" (Phinney, 1992). The overall score is obtained by reversing negatively worded items, adding across items, and by calculating the mean (Phinney, 1992).

As a result of testing 136 college students (Asian, Black, Hispanic, White, and Mixed), Phinney (1992) argues that ethnic identity becomes more defined with age. Further, Phinney found that attitudes toward others were unrelated to ethnic identity, ethnic identity achievement was more visible among older students, and self-esteem (measured with ethnic identity) was statistically significant for Minority students but not for the White students. Phinney contends that the scores for Whites will increase in the area of ethnic identity once they have more exposure of being the Minority in specific settings.

Ethnic Identity Development of White Americans and Their Perceptions of Self and Others

Unlike the racial development of Blacks and Minorities, Whites go through the following five stages of racial identity development:

1. **Contact.** The individual is either curious or is in trepidation about Blacks, and has a lack of awareness of being White.
2. **Disintegration.** An individual experiences guilt and anxiety and becomes aware of the social implications of race on a personal level.
3. **Reintegration.** The individual believes that White people are superior to people of color.
4. **Pseudo-independent.** The individual begins to define a positive White identity and abandon racism.
5. **Autonomy.** Individuals accept racial differences and value cultural diversity.

According to Block, Roberson, and Neuger, the developmental tasks for White individuals are to "recognize and overcome institutional and cultural racism, abandon individual racism, and develop a positive, nonracist White identity." This process of White racial identity takes form in five stages. The contact stage characterizes White individuals as having limited contact with Blacks either within work environment or social environments. These individuals have a tendency to judge Blacks by White standards of academic testing and the use of the English language (Block, Roberson, and Neuger, 1992).

The stage of disintegration labels the White individual as either experiencing guilt or anxiety toward Blacks, which is motivated by White racism. To reconcile with the internal conflict, the White individual chooses one of two options: He increases contact with Blacks at work and socially, or the White individual adopts the notion the White racism is justified because Blacks are inferior to Whites (Block, Roberson, and Neuger, 1992).

At the reintegration stage, the White individual is hostile toward Blacks and believes that individual and cultural racism against Blacks is a form of power and privilege that Whites have earned (Block, Roberson, and Neuger, 1992). The White individual at the pseudo-independent stage attempts to take on a more positive White identity in helping Blacks become more "White" to better survive White culture (Block, Roberson, and Neuger, 1992). And, once the individual reaches the stage of autonomy, he or she is interested in learning more about the racial and cultural differences among Whites and Blacks, and the White individual is more concerned about changing the behavior of Whites as opposed to changing the behaviors of Blacks (Block, Roberson, and Neuger, 1992).

In Block, Roberson, and Neuger's study, Helm's model of racial identity was used to predict how individual differences in racial identity attitudes, specifically Whites', would influence attitudes toward diversity in organizations. Block, Roberson, Neuger argue that it is racial identity, not race, which influences interracial behavior. To assess managerial attitudes toward workforce diversity issues, Block, Roberson, and Neuger (1992) created a questionnaire consisting of four scales:

- supporting principles of workforce diversity (seven items)
- perceptions of the environment (ten items)
- beliefs about implementation
- workplace social distance

Based on regression and correlation analyses, all four scales were statistically significant. Findings indicate that White racial identity attitudes predict managers' perceptions toward supporting principles of workforce diversity, perceptions of the work environment as being equitable, and beliefs about which implementation steps are necessary toward achieving workforce diversity goals (Block, Roberson, and Neuger, 1992).

The results of this study indicate that change in White racial identity may affect perceptions of the success of workforce diversity efforts. Results cited earlier suggest that the perceptions of Blacks also change with the level of ethnic identity development. Thus, the present study will explore ethnic identity development and the differences of perceived leader diversity acceptance, and how desirable the leader is to work for, among White and Black workers.

Management and Its Influence on Workplace Diversity

According to Thomas, Black workers are becoming increasingly aware of the unfulfilled promises of assimilation (Thomas, 1991). Despite the fact that Black workers leave who they are at the door and take on a different persona, which is more palatable to Whites, they continue to find themselves at the bottom of the organization. Those that do advance within the organization find themselves confronted by the "glass ceiling" (Thomas, 1991). Yet, Black workers are told on a regular basis that their lack of and or limited career development has nothing to do with the color of their skin (Bonacich, 1992). Needless to say, Black workers have developed a different perception than their White counterparts of "who" is allowed to be successful in White establishments. Thomas contends that both White and Black workers are entering the workplace with diverse perceptions based on race and color. If different perceptions occur, it becomes important to understand what systematic differences exist so that management may address them appropriately.

Thomas refers to three management styles that can either inhibit or promote diversity management within the workplace (Affirmative Action strategies, valuing differences strategies, and diversity management strategies). The first management style, Affirmative Action, rests on the notion that systemic racism can be remedied through attracting and promoting Blacks within the workplace. Although this approach may acknowledge that some changes should be made in upper management to reflect a more harmonious work environment, little is suggested to make such changes (Thomas, 1991). Thomas contends that managers who rely on Affirmative Action tactics are concerned with ridding the organization of expressions of blatant racism and sexism. They are content with creating a work environment that is "color-blind," "race-blind" and "gender-blind" (Thomas, 1991). These managers are interested in recruiting Black workers and are supportive of programs that will assist Blacks with the assimilation process. However, they do not take the initiative to work toward organizational change that would ultimately effect the upward mobility of Blacks (advancing beyond the glass ceiling) (Thomas, 1991).

In the second management style (valuing differences) the leader exhibits consciousness about the diverse workforce and is preoccupied with making sure that Minorities within the workplace are recognized for their differences. Such recognition is brought about through workshops and activities (Thomas, 1991). Managers who promote valuing differences programs bring about some sense of awareness of gender, race, and sexual orientation differences. This awareness is believed to improve interpersonal relationships among workers (Thomas, 1991).

Corporate America is attempting to improve interracial relations among Black and White workers through diversity awareness and valuing differences workshops. However, the issue of how to deconstruct White racism in an effort to empower Blacks as a group and improve race relations is not directly addressed by these workshops. Within such workshops, Black participants usually take on the victim role while blaming Whites for the ill-effects they've experienced through White racism (Thomas, 1991). Although these feelings are justified, the group members rarely move beyond the racial tension that exists between the two racial groups, and the work of accepting differences goes unfinished (Thomas, 1991). This leads Thomas (1991) to the conclusion that the racial perceptions held by both White and Black workers will have to be more clearly understood. This is especially true of the difference in perception of diversity acceptance itself and of the assumptions used in creating effective organizations.

Thus, the third management style (diversity management) challenges the organization's fundamental assumptions about human relations. In addition, it takes the initiative to question the relationships between workers, managers, and the establishment (Thomas, 1991). Managers using diversity management question personal and institutional assumptions. These managers are also interested in cultivating the talents of all their workers.

The creation of a heterogeneous work environment that taps into the full potential of all its employees and includes the workers in the decision-making processes is an initiative that management must take if it is to effectively manage today's workforce (Thomas, 1991, 1996).

Rationale and Hypotheses of This Study

The process of learning about race is part of a child's everyday experience as he or she acquires knowledge about his- or herself and the society (Clark, 1963). Although the cognitive processes for determining one's ethnic identity are more sophisticated for adults than for children, the fundamental beliefs about who we are as individuals, group members, and as "others" can be modeled in a system of ethnic identity development (Rotheram, and Phinney, 1987). Patterns of privilege in the United States make the ethnic identity development process different for Minorities and for Whites (Rotheram and Phinney, 1987). These different patterns of identity development interact with biases created by intergroup relations (Tajfel, 1982). Hence, adult workers bring with them into the workplace biased beliefs about others that interfere with the work of resolving diversity issues (Bonacich, 1992). Our race, ethnic identity development, group membership, and biases influence our experiences and perceptions of self and others with respect to race (Allport, 1979). These differences in self and other perceptions affect workplace perceptions of diversity acceptance. Different people are likely to believe that very different approaches to diversity at work are warranted (Thomas, 1991). In addition, leaders' approaches to diversity are likely to affect differently worker's perceptions of the desirability of the leaders. Therefore, the following predictions about ethnicity, ethnic identity development, diversity acceptance by leader, and desirability to work for a leader have been made.

Hypothesis 1

Hypothesis 1a. Respondents will assess Scenario Three leaders as more accepting of diversity than leaders in Scenarios One (Affirmative Action) and Two (valuing diversity).

Hypothesis 1b. Respondents will assess Scenario Three leaders as more desirable to work for than leaders in Scenarios One (Affirmative Action) and Two (valuing diversity).

Based on Thomas' argument for diversity management, workers are growing tired of assimilation and are seeking out organizations that will accept them as unique individuals. Thomas suggests that diversity management and valuing diversity strategies are more expansive and accepting of unique individuals than affirmative action strategies (Thomas, 1991). Thus, it is predicted here that Thomas' diversity management approach will generally be seen as more accepting of diversity.

Hypothesis 2

Ethnicity of respondent will be the moderating variable in the relationship of perceived diversity acceptance of the leader and perceived desirability to work for the leader.

Specifically, Black respondents will report greater correlation of diversity acceptance and leader desirability ratings than White respondents. This prediction is based on studies that show that people of color find diversity initiatives at work more important and desirable than Whites (Alderfer, 1982; Bonacich, 1992; Henderson, 1994; Yamato, 1992).

Hypothesis 3

Ethnic identity development of the respondent will be a moderating variable in the relationship of perceived diversity acceptance of the leader and perceived desirability to work for the leader. Specifically, respondents with a high degree of ethnic identity development will report greater correlation of diversity acceptance and leader desirability ratings than respondents with a low degree of ethnic identity development.

This prediction is supported by Block, Roberson, and Neuger (1992). White individuals who score high on the levels of autonomy, pseudo-independent, and contact are more likely to be accepting and supportive of diversity initiatives within the workplace than White individuals who score low on these dimensions (Block, Roberson, and Neuger, 1992).

Hypothesis 4

Hypothesis 4a. Ethnicity and ethnic identity development of the respondent will interact as moderating variables in the relationship of perceived diversity acceptance of the leader. Specifically, relationship to diversity acceptance will array in order of highest to lowest for: a) Black respondents with high ethnic identity; b) White respondents with high ethnic identity next; c) Black respondents with low ethnic identity next; d) White respondents with low ethnic identity (having the least covariance of diversity acceptance and leader desirability).

Hypothesis 4b. Ethnicity and ethnic identity development of the respondent will interact as moderating variables in the relationship of perceived desirability of the leader. Specifically, relationship to leader desirability will array in order of highest to lowest for: a) Black respondents with high ethnic identity; b) White respondents with high ethnic identity; c) Black respondents with low ethnic identity; d) White respondents with low ethnic identity (again having the least covariance of diversity acceptance and leader desirability).

Hypothesis 5

Leaders who are perceived as having a high level of acceptance of diversity will be judged as more desirable to work for than leaders who are perceived as having a lower level of acceptance of diversity.

Based on Thomas' argument for diversity management, workers are more likely to make full contributions if leaders are accepting of diversity than for a leader that is non-accepting of diversity (Thomas, 1996). Thus, workers will find such leaders more desirable to work for.

Hypothesis 6

White leaders who are perceived as having a high degree of acceptance of diversity will be judged more desirable to work for than Black leaders who are perceived to have a high degree of acceptance of diversity.

It is believed that acceptance by White leaders will be perceived as more indicative of change in the previously White culture of the organization than acceptance of Black leaders (Berg, 1984). Thus, workers will view a White leader who has accepted diversity as more desirable to work for than a Black leader who has accepted diversity.

These hypotheses address the issue of ethnic identity development of Blacks and Whites and its affects on perceptions of leaders' definitions of managing diversity within the workplace. Within the workplace there can be said to be three strategic styles in managing diversity: Affirmative Action, valuing differences, and managing diversity (Thomas, 1991). Jamieson and O'Mara (1991) contend that workers and managers need to be more flexible in their beliefs, styles, values, and practices as they are confronted with the task of managing today's diverse workforce. Such inflexibility coupled with one's ethnicity and ethnic identity development, may influence perceptions of who one feels most comfortable working for and how accepting others (especially leaders) are of diversity at work (Block, Roberson, and Neuger, 1992). As managers attempt to utilize more than one management style to manage their work and the diverse issues that exist among White and Black workers, they will soon come to realize that diversity means acknowledging cultural differences with respect to "the nature of time, human relationships, reality and truth, space and human activity" (Jamieson and O'Mara, 1991). White and Black workers bring to

31

the work environment their ethnicity and various perceptions, which influence their interpretations of diversity implementations and values at work (Rotheram and Phinney, 1987; Phinney, 1992).

Chapter III
Methods

Participants

An exploratory survey was conducted to measure diversity acceptance and the desirability of working for leaders with various diversity approaches. Two hundred workers, an approximate equal number of Black males and females and White males and females, were surveyed at several retail stores. In an effort to increase the response rate, the researcher surveyed workers outside of their place of employment. Volunteers were not paid for their participation.

Process

Each participant was given two survey instruments. First, each respondent was asked to read and respond to each of the fourteen items on Multigroup Ethnic Identity Measure (MEIM) (Phinney, 1992). Second, each respondent was asked to read and evaluate a three-scenario survey of diversity acceptance and leader desirability scenarios.

Multigroup Ethnic Identity Measure (MEIM) Scale

The MEIM is based on research of children, adolescent, and adult ethnic identity development (Phinney, 1987, 1989, 1992,1993). Phinney's Multigroup Ethnic Identity Measure (MEIM) has two factors of self identification: ethnic identity and other group orientation, both representing issues that are common within the ethnic identity development of all ethnic groups.

The MEIM consists of fourteen items which are divided into three subscales: a) affirmation and belonging; b) ethnic identity achievement; and c) ethnic behaviors. Individuals rate the items by using a four-point scale from "strongly agree" to "strongly disagree" (Phinney, 1992). The overall score is obtained by reversing negatively worded items, adding across items, and by calculating the mean (Phinney, 1992). The open-ended questions that address ethnic self-identification and parents' ethnicity are not scored but are used to provide background information (Phinney, 1992).

In Phinney's study, the overall reliability of the scale was 81 percent (high school sample) and 90 percent (college sample); the sense of belonging scale was 75 percent (high school sample) and 86 percent (college sample); the ethnic identity achievement scale was 69 percent (high school sample) and 80 percent (college sample); and there were no coefficients for the two-item scale of ethnic behavior. As a result of testing 136 college students (Asian, Black, Hispanic, White, and Mixed), Phinney (1992) argues that ethnic identity becomes more defined with age. In addition, attitudes toward others was unrelated to ethnic identity and ethnic identity achievement was more visible among the older students. Further, self-esteem (measured with ethnic identity) was statistically significant for the Minority students, but not for the White students.

The MEIM measure created for this study was influenced by Phinney's (1992) MEIM measure. The first fourteen items of Phinney's measure focus on three aspects of ethnic identity:

- positive ethnic attitudes and sense of belonging
- ethnic identity achievement
- ethnic behaviors or practices

For the purpose of this study, the categories remained the same, but the wording of those fourteen items was rephrased. In addition, several items were not used from Phinney's (1992) MEIM due to their irrelevant areas of focus. Items fifteen through twenty focus on other group orientation, and items twenty-two and twenty-three focus on parents' ethnicity. The reliability of the overall scale was 58 percent.

Leader Diversity Acceptance and Desirability

The researcher created scenarios out of Thomas' (1991) three management styles for diversity. Each survey has scenarios addressing diversity issues in each of the styles suggested by Thomas (1991):

- Affirmative Action (a legal initiative based on the Civil Rights Act of 1969 that seeks to prevent discrimination because of race, gender, age, disability, religion, or national origin);
- valuing differences (the creation of a work environment that promotes understanding and respect of group differences);
- managing diversity (managing a diverse workforce to tap into full human potential).

Affirmative Action

Scenario One focuses on a manager's belief that the recruitment of Minority workers into entry- level positions is necessary for the advancement of diversity within the workplace (Thomas, 1996). Thomas states that this is typical of Affirmative Action. Managers of Affirmative Action utilize recruiting techniques to increase the number of Minority and Women workers.

Valuing Differences

Scenario Two focuses on recognition of the differences as well as the similarities that exist among workers through awareness workshops and the promotion of organization involvement in ethnic holidays and activities. Thus, Thomas argues that celebrating ethnic holidays is typical of "valuing differences." Valuing differences is also concerned with improving interpersonal relationships within the workplace through awareness workshops (Thomas, 1996).

Managing Diversity

Scenario Three focuses on an organization's attempt to assess the needs of its diverse workforce. In taking the necessary measures to collect data and to involve the workers by requesting their input (opinion surveys), top management is taking a stand to manage the diversity that exists among all of its workers, including the White male worker. This is what Thomas refers to as "diversity management." Managers who are interested in managing their diverse workforce are interested in tapping into the full potential of their employees, as well as addressing issues and concerns about the organization itself, which prevents employees from making a full contribution (Thomas, 1996). In addition they show concern for creating inclusive structures.

Each scenario in the measure created for this study is attributed to either a White or Black leader. There are two versions of the survey, in which the ordering of White and Black leaders is varied. Thus, each scenario differs in context and race of the leader. For example, the scenarios for the first version are as follows: Scenario One is a statement from a White leader; Scenario Two is a statement from a Black leader; and Scenario Three is a statement from a White leader. The scenarios for the second version are the following: Scenario One is a statement from a Black leader; Scenario Two is a statement from a White leader; and scenario Three is a statement from a Black leader. The gender of the White and Black leaders is anonymous to eliminate gender effects.

For the purpose of identifying each version of the survey and to expedite data entry, the surveys were printed on two different colors. Respondents were randomly assigned to one of the two versions of the survey.

Each scenario is followed by two seven-point Likert scales:

1. Diversity acceptance
2. Desirability to work for

The scale "acceptance of diversity" measured an individual's perception of the leader's diversity acceptance within the workplace from "non-accepting" to "extremely accepting." The scale "desirability to work for" measured an individual's positive or negative preference of working for the leader in each scenario from "extremely undesirable" to "extremely desirable."

This measure also included a short demographic section. The demographic items included: ethnicity, gender, age, years with organization, and type of position held within the organization. Although this study focused on White and Black subjects, the ethnicity of response included all other ethnic groups to eliminate response bias. The reliability of this scale is 71 percent.

Data Analysis Procedures

Given the nature of the hypotheses and complexity of the survey forms, data were organized into two types of data analyses sets. One ordered data by leader ethnicity and leader diversity strategy- -"leader." The other ordered data by respondent ethnicity and respondent ethnic identity development—"respondent."

Hypothesis 1

Hypothesis 1a. Respondents will assess Scenario Three leaders as more accepting of diversity than leaders in Scenarios One (Affirmative Action) and Two (valuing diversity).

Hypothesis 1b. Respondents will assess Scenario Three leaders as more desirable to work for than leaders in Scenarios One (Affirmative Action) and Two (valuing diversity).

These were tested by using the first form of data analysis set (leader). Acceptance ratings for all scenarios depicting the managing diversity style (Scenario Three leader) were summed and a mean acceptance rating was calculated. Similarly, desirability ratings for all other scenarios were summed and a mean was determined. Two independent (t-tests) between Scenario Three leaders and all others were calculated. For Hypothesis 1a, a t-test assessed the mean score differences in acceptance between all Scenario Three leaders and all Scenario One and Two leaders. For hypothesis 1b, a t-test assessed the mean score differences in desirability of Scenario Three and other leaders.

Hypothesis 2

Ethnicity of subject will be a moderating variable in the relationship of perceived diversity acceptance of leader and perceived desirability of leader. Specifically, Black respondents will report greater relationship of diversity acceptance and leader desirability ratings than White respondents.

Tests of Hypothesis 2 used the second type of data analysis set (respondent). Difference scores were calculated between acceptance and desirability scores across all scenarios for each respondent. Respondents were divided into Blacks and Whites. A t-test was conducted between Black and White respondent groups.

Hypothesis 3

Ethnic identity development of respondent will be a moderating variable in the relationship of perceived diversity acceptance of leader and perceived desirability of leader. Specifically, respondents with a high degree of ethnic identity development will report a greater relationship of diversity acceptance and leader desirability ratings than respondents with a low degree of ethnic identity development.

This was tested with the second type of data analysis set. Respondents were divided into groups of high and low on total scores of ethnic identity development (calculated as instructed by Phinney, 1992). Difference scores between acceptance and desirability rating for respondents were calculated and summed by respondent. A one-way (ANOVA) was calculated for ethnicity by differences score.

Hypothesis 4

Hypothesis 4a. Ethnicity and ethnic identity development of respondent will interact as moderating variables in the relationship of perceived diversity acceptance of leader. Specifically, correlation of diversity acceptance and leader desirability will array in order of highest to lowest correlation for:

38

- Black respondents with high ethnic identity
- White respondents with high ethnic identity
- Black respondents with low ethnic identity
- White respondents with low ethnic identity

The last category's members have the least covariance of diversity acceptance and leader desirability.

Hypothesis 4b. Ethnicity and ethnic identity development of respondent will interact as moderating variables in the relationship of perceived desirability of leader. Specifically, correlation of diversity acceptance and leader desirability will array in order of highest to lowest correlation for:

- Black respondents with high ethnic identity
- White respondents with high ethnic identity
- Black respondents with low ethnic identity
- White respondents with low ethnic identity (again having the least covariance of diversity acceptance and leader desirability)

Both hypotheses were tested by a two-way ANOVA to measure the interaction effect between acceptance and desirability.

Hypothesis 5

Leaders who are perceived to have accepted diversity will be judged as more desirable to work for than leaders who are not perceived as having accepted diversity.

Total acceptance scores of leaders in each scenario were calculated by summing all respondent acceptance scores in each scenario and finding a mean acceptance score for each scenario leader. Similarly, total desirability scores of leaders in each scenario were calculated by summing all respondents desirability scores in each scenario and finding a mean desirability score for each scenario leader. A Pearson R^2 was conducted to determine the correlation between acceptance and desirability to work for a leader.

Hypothesis 6

White leaders who are perceived as having accepted diversity will be judged more desirable to work for than Black leaders who are perceived to have accepted diversity.

The group of leaders judged as having high acceptance of diversity were broken down further into Black and White leader groups. Interaction effects in a two-way ANOVA were used to determine the interaction on ethnicity and high and low acceptance or desirability to work for a leader.

Chapter IV

Results

Hypothesis 1

Hypothesis 1a. Respondents will assess Scenario Three leaders as more accepting of diversity than leaders in Scenarios One (Affirmative Action) and Two (valuing differences).

Using the first set of data analysis (leader), acceptance ratings for all scenario leaders depicting the managing diversity style (Scenario Three leaders) were summed and a mean acceptance rating was calculated. A paired t-test was conducted to assess the mean-score differences in acceptance between all Scenario One, Two, and Three leaders. The results showed a significant difference: t (-22.902), p .000. Scenario Three leaders were rated as having a significantly higher acceptance of diversity (M = 6.01) than Scenario One and Two leaders (M = 4.09) (*see* Table 4.1). Thus, these data support Hypothesis 1a.

Hypothesis 1b. Respondents will assess Scenario Three leaders as more desirable to work for than leaders in Scenarios One (Affirmative Action) and Two (valuing differences).

Using the first set of data analysis (leader), desirability ratings for all scenario leaders depicting the managing diversity style (Scenario Three leaders) were summed and a mean desirability rating was calculated. A paired t-test was conducted to assess the mean score differences in desirability between all Scenario One, Two, and Three leaders. The results showed a significant difference, t (-24.434), p .000. Scenario Three leaders were rated as being significantly more desirable to work for (M = 6.21) Scenario One and Two leaders (M = 4.33) (see Table 4.2). Thus, these data support Hypothesis 1b.

Table 4.1

Paired t-test: Mean of acceptance of Scenario One and Two leaders compared with mean acceptance of Scenario Three leaders.

	Mean	N	Std. Dev.	Std. EM	Paired Differences					
					Mean	Std. Dev.	Std. EM	t	df	Sig
Pair Sum of 1&2 1 Leaders acceptance	4.0900	200	.9388	6.6E-02						
Scenario 3 Leaders acceptance	6.01	200	.75	5.39E-02	-1.9200	1.1856	8.4E-02	-22.902	199	.000

Table 4.2

Paired t-test: Mean of desirability to work for of Scenario One and Two leaders compared with mean desirability of Scenario Three leaders.

	Mean	N	Std. Dev.	Std. EM	Paired Differences					
					Mean	Std. Dev.	Std. EM	t	df	Sig
Pair Sum of 1&2 1 Leaders desirability	4.3350	200	.9107	6.4E-02						
Scenario 3 Leaders desirability	6.21	200	.69	4.88E-02	-1.8700	1.0823	7.7E-02	-24.434	199	.000

Hypothesis 2

Ethnicity of respondent will be a moderating variable in the relationship of perceived diversity acceptance of leader and perceived desirability of leader. Specifically, Black respondents will report a greater relationship of diversity of acceptance and leader desirability ratings than White respondents.

The second form set of data analysis (respondent) was divided into Black and White respondents and difference scores were calculated between acceptance and desirability scores across all scenarios for each respondent. The results of an independent t-test showed no significant difference for ethnicity on relationship acceptance and desirability scores $F(.032), p = .859$ (see Table 4.3). Thus, Hypothesis 2 was not supported.

Hypothesis 3

Ethnic identity development (EID) of respondent will be a moderating variable in the relationship of perceived diversity acceptance of leader and perceived desirability of leader. Specifically, respondents with a high degree of EID will report a greater relationship of diversity acceptance and leader desirability to work for.

The second set of data (respondent) was divided into groups of high and low on total scores of EID (calculated as instructed by Phinney, 1992). The results of a one-way ANOVA showed no significance for EID on diversity acceptance and desirability to work for a leader $F(.050), P = .824$ (see Table 4.4). Thus, these data do not support Hypothesis 3.

Hypothesis 4

Hypothesis 4a. Ethnicity and EID of respondent will interact as moderating variables in relationship to perceived diversity acceptance of leader. Specifically, relationship to diversity acceptance will array in order of highest to lowest for:

- Black respondents with high ethnic identity
- White respondents with high ethnic identity

43

Table 4.3

Independent t-test: Ethnicity as it relates to perceived difference between diversity acceptance and desirability to work for.

Leven's Test for Equality of Variance

	Respondent's ethnicity	N	Mean	Std. Dev.	Std. EM	F	Sig.	t	df	Sig (2-tailed)	Mean Diff.	Std. Er.D.
Differences in acceptance desirability scores of leaders	Black	100	-.7400	.7333	7.3E-02							
	White	100	-.6300	.7475	7.5E-02							
Equal variances assumed						.032	.859	-1.050	198	.295	-.1100	.1047

Table 4.4

One-way ANOVA: EID as it relates to perceived difference between diversity acceptance and desirability to work for.

	Respondent's EID Scores	N	Mean	Std. Dev.	Std. Error	Sum of squares	df	Mean square	F	Sig.
Difference in acceptance desirability scores	low	123	-.6911	.7802	7.0E-02					
	high	75	-.6667	.6844	7.9E-02					
		198	-.6818	.7437	5.3E-02					
	(Total Between Groups)					2.8E-02	1	2.8E-02	.050	.824

- Black respondents with low ethnic identity
- White respondents with low ethnic identity (having the least co-variance of diversity acceptance)

An initial two-way ANOVA measuring the interaction effect between the full EID score and ethnicity in relationship to perceived diversity acceptance indicated a significant interaction, F (6.677), p .011. Black respondents with high EID (M = 13.97), White respondents with high EID (M = 14), Black respondents with low EID (M = 13.43), White respondents with low EID (M = 14.97) (see Table 4.5). Thus, Hypothesis 4a was partially supported. The ordering of groups was not as expected. First were White respondents with low EID, then White respondents with high EID, next Black respondents with high EID, and Black respondents with low EID.

Hypothesis 4b. Ethnicity and EID of respondent will interact as moderating variables in relationship to perceived desirability of leader. Specifically, relationship to leader desirability will array in order of highest to lowest for:

- Black respondents with high ethnic identity
- White respondents with high ethnic identity
- Black respondents with low ethnic identity
- White respondents with low ethnic identity (having the least co-variance of leader desirability)

An initial two-way ANOVA measuring the interaction effect, between the full EID score and ethnicity in relationship to perceived desirability of leader, indicated a significant interaction: F (7.335), p .007. White respondents had low EID (M = 15.62), Black respondents had high EID (M = 14.7), White respondents had high EID (M = 14.57), Black respondents had low EID (M = 14.17). (see Table 4.6). Thus, these data partially support Hypothesis 4b. The ordering of groups was not as expected. First were White respondents with high EID, then Black respondents with low EID, next White respondents with high EID, and Black respondents with low EID.

Given that the reliability for the MEIM scale is 58 percent, a post-hoc test was conducted on the MEIM scale to further investigate the items that contributed to the statistical insignificance of Hypothesis 3 and the significance of Hypotheses 4a and 4b. As a result of running an inter-item corre-

Table 4.5

Two-way ANOVA: Two-way interaction of diversity acceptance with ethnicity and EID.

		Sum of Squares	df	Mean Square	F	Sig.	Mean scores of total acceptance low /high
Total Acceptance	Main Effects (Combined)	33.913	2	16.957	4.437	.013	
	Ethnicity & EID scores (high/low)	26.968	1	26.968	7.056	.009	
		1.995	1	1.995	.522	.471	
Two-Way Interactions	Ethnicity & EID scores (high/low)	25.518	1	25.518	6.677	.011	
							(Black) 13.43 13.97
							(White) 14.97 14.00

Table 4.6

Two-way ANOVA: Two-way interaction of desirability with ethnicity and EID.

		Sum of Squares	df	Mean Square	F	Sig.		Mean scores of total desirability low/high	
Total Desirability	Main Effects (Combined)	27.039	2	13.520	3.598	.029			
	Ethnicity &	19.192	1	19.192	5.108	.025			
	EID scores (high/low)	3.080	1	3.080	.820	.366			
	Ethnicity &	27.561	1	27.561	7.335	.007			
Two-Way Interactions	EID scores (high/low)								
							(Black)	14.17	14.70
							(White)	15.62	14.57

lation, items 7, 8, and 10 were taken out of the scale due to their low mean scores as compared to the other 11 items on the scale. The weakness within these items may be due to their negative wording. In reading items 7, 8, and 10, respondents may have responded to them as if they were positive items, thus confusing the respondents. Once the items were omitted, a reliability analysis was performed on the MEIM scale. Interestingly enough, the reliability of the scale increased to 73 percent. With such an increase in the reliability level, Hypotheses 3 and 4 were also tested again to see if the revised scale would create a difference in their statistical significance.

Hypothesis 3 (revised)

Ethnic identity development (EID) of respondent will be a moderating variable in the relationship of perceived diversity acceptance of leader and perceived desirability of leader. Specifically, respondents with a high degree of EID will report a greater relationship of diversity acceptance and desirability to work for the leader.

The second set of data (respondent) was divided into groups of high and low on total scores of EID (calculated as instructed by Phinney, 1992). The results of a one-way ANOVA showed no significance for EID on diversity acceptance and desirability to work for the leader, $F(.023)$, $p=.878$ (see Table 4.7). Thus, these data do not support Hypothesis 3.

Hypothesis 4 (revised)

Hypothesis 4a (revised). Ethnicity and EID of respondent will interact as moderating variables in relationship to perceived diversity acceptance of leader. Specifically, relationship to diversity acceptance will array in order of highest to lowest for

- Black respondents with high ethnic identity
- White respondents with high ethnic identity
- Black respondents with low ethnic identity
- White respondents with low ethnic identity (having the least covariance of diversity acceptance).

48

Table 4.7

One-way ANOVA: EID as it relates to perceived difference between diversity acceptance and desirability to work for (revised MEIM scale).

Respondents EID scores		N	Mean	Std. Dev.	Std. Error
Difference in acceptance vs. desirability scores	low	58	-.6724	.8663	.1137
	high	142	-.6901	.6861	5.8E-02
	Total	200	-.6850	.7406	5.2E-02

	Sum of squares	df	Mean square	F	Sig.
(Between Groups)	1.3E-02	1	.551	.023	.878

A two-way ANOVA measuring the interaction effect between EID and ethnicity in relationship to perceived diversity acceptance did not indicate a significant interaction: F (3.036), $p = .083$. (see Table 4.8). Thus, these data do not support Hypothesis 4a (revised).

Hypothesis 4b (revised). Ethnicity and EID of respondent will interact as moderating variables in relationship to perceived desirability of leader. Specifically, relationship to leader desirability will array in order of highest to lowest for:

- Black respondents with high ethnic identity
- White respondents with high ethnic identity
- Black respondents with low ethnic identity
- White respondents with low ethnic identity

A two-way ANOVA measuring the interaction effect between EID and ethnicity in relationship to perceived desirability of leader indicated an insignificant interaction: F (2.957), $p = .087$ (see Table 4.9). Thus, these data do not support Hypothesis 4b (revised).

Hypothesis 5

Leaders who are perceived to have a high level of diversity acceptance will be judged as more desirable to work for than leaders who are perceived to have a low level of diversity acceptance.

Total acceptance scores of leaders in each scenario were calculated by summing all respondents acceptance scores in each scenario and finding a mean acceptance score for each scenario leader. Similarly, total desirability scores of leaders in each scenario were calculated by summing all respondents' desirability scores in each scenario and finding a mean desirability score for each scenario leader.

The results of a Pearson R2 showed a significant correlation between high and low acceptance group differences on perceived desirability to work for: $R2$ (.933), p .000 (see Table 4.10). Thus, Hypothesis 5 was supported.

Table 4.8

Two-way ANOVA: Two-way interaction of diversity acceptance with Ethnicity and EID (revised MEIM scale).

		Sum of Squares	df	Mean Square	F	Sig	Mean scores of Total acceptance low/high	
Total Main effects	(Combined)	74.509	2	37.254	9.686	.000		
	Ethnicity & EID scores	48.511	1	48.511	12.613	.000		
		5.447	1	5.447	1.416	.235		
Two-way Interactions	Ethnicity & EID scores	11.676	1	11.676	3.036	.083		
							(Black) 13.52	13.71
							(White) 14.31	15.26

Table 4.9

Two-way ANOVA: Two-way interaction of desirability with Ethnicity and EID (revised MEIM scale).

		Sum of Squares	df	Mean Square	F	Sig.	Mean scores of total desirability low/high	
Total Desirability	Main Effects (Combined)	63.604	2	31.802	8.385	.000		
	Ethnicity & EID scores (high/low)	39.104	1	39.104	10.310	.002		
		5.971	1	5.971	1.574	.211		
Two-Way Interactions	Ethnicity & EID scores (high/low)	11.217	1	11.217	2.957	.087		
							(Black) 14.29	14.44
							(White) 15.90	14.93

Table 4.10

Pearson R2: Correlation of total acceptance and total desirability scores of leaders.

		Total acceptance	Total desirability
Pearson Correlation	Total acceptance	1.000	.933**
	Total desirability	.933**	1.000
Sig	Total acceptance		.000
	Total desirability	.000	
N	Total acceptance	200	200
	Total desirability	200	200

Hypothesis 6

White leaders who are perceived as having accepted diversity will be judged more desirable to work for than Black leaders who are perceived to have accepted diversity.

The group of leaders judged as having high acceptance of diversity were broken down further into high Black and White leader groups by scenarios (One, Two, and Three). Interaction effects in a two-way ANOVA showed no significant interaction in ethnicity and acceptance for desirability: F (.378), $p = .539$ (see Table 4.11). Thus, Hypothesis 6 was not supported.

Table 4.11

Two-way ANOVA: Two-way interaction of desirability by ethnicity and acceptance.

			Sum of Squares	df	Mean Square	F	Sig.
Total desirability	Main Effects	(Combined)	478.475	2	239.237	142.794	.000
		Ethnicity	4.722	1	4.722	2.819	.095
		Acceptance (high/low)	435.282	1	435.282	259.807	.000
	Two-Way Interactions	Ethnicity Acceptance (high/low)	.633	1	.633	.378	.539

Chapter V
Discussion

Based on Thomas' argument in 1991 argument for diversity management, workers are growing tired of assimilation and are seeking out organizations that will accept them as unique individuals. Thomas suggests that diversity management and valuing diversity strategies are more expansive and accepting of unique individuals than Affirmative Action strategies (Thomas, 1991). Thus, it was predicted here that Thomas' diversity management approach would generally be seen as more accepting of diversity.

This study found that indeed, respondents did rate Scenario Three leaders as more accepting of diversity and more desirable to work for than Scenario One and Two leaders. The Affirmative Action leader (Scenario One) associated corporate success with assimilation and quotas. On the other hand, the valuing differences leader (Scenario Two) takes on a neutral stance in not taking opportunities from one group to provide for another, but attempts to educate its workers about cultural differences through awareness programs. Unlike Scenario One and Two leaders, managing diversity leader (Scenario Three) is interested in the quality of work life of all its workers. It is important to note that the most recent legal initiatives against Affirmative Action may dull the awareness of existing institutional racism. White and Black workers, specifically Black workers, might expect to not only work for organizations that do not acknowledge their ethnicity and color, but be unwilling to provide an open forum for discussing perceived feelings of discrimination. The managing diversity leader's approach to addressing diversity within the workplace may be representative of workers seeking from their employers: fairness, inclusion, and opportunity.

Previous studies show that people of color find diversity initiatives at work more important and desirable than Whites (Alderfer, 1982; Bonacich, 1992; Henderson, 1994; and Yamato, 1992). Thus, in this study it was predicted that respondents of color would report greater correlation of diversity acceptance and leader desirability ratings than would White subjects. This was not found to be the case in this study. Based on the response rates, the ethnicity of the Black and White respondents did not appear to affect their perceptions of diversity acceptance and leader desirability to work for. This may be because there was such a high correspondence of desirability and acceptance ratings in general: R2 (.933). However, it should be noted that this high correspondence could have been the result of the two scales being placed next to one another on the survey.

Block, Roberson, and Neuger found that White individuals who score high on the levels of autonomy, pseudo-independent, and contact in EID are more likely to be accepting of and supportive of diversity initiatives within the workplace than White individuals who score low on these dimensions. An individual's perception of self and others is rooted in racial identity, and one's ethnic identity influences how we feel and behave towards one another (Black, Roberson, and Neuger, 1992). Thus, it was predicted that ethnic identity development of respondents would be a moderating variable in the relationship of perceived diversity acceptance of leader and perceived desirability of leader. The results from this study did not support earlier findings.

On the other hand, previous studies suggest that ethnicity and ethnic identity development (EID) may affect racial relationships (Williams, Morland, 1976; and Rotheram and Phinney, 1987). These assumptions lead to the prediction that ethnicity and EID of respondents would interact as moderating variables in relationship to scores of perceived diversity acceptance and scores of perceived desirability of the leader. This study did not support this prediction. Though initial tests of Hypotheses 4a and 4b did show some relationship between EID, ethnicity and leader diversity acceptance and desirability to work for this was based on use of the full MEIM scale, which only had a reliability of 58 percent. Thus, a post-hoc test was conducted on the MEIM scale to further investigate the items on the MEIM scale that contributed to the statistical insignificance of Hypothesis 3, and the significance of Hypotheses 4a and 4b. As a result of running an inter-item correlation, items 7, 8, and 10 were taken out of the scale due to their low mean scores as compared to the other 11 items on the scale. With the omission of these items the reliability of the scale increased to 73 percent. With such an increase in the reliability level, Hypotheses 3 and 4 were also re-tested to see if the revised scale would create a difference in their statistical significance. Hypothesis 3 remained statistically insignificant; however, Hypotheses 4a and 4b changed from statistically significant to insignificant.

With most of the policy and decision makers in corporate America being predominantly White, initiatives taken to manage today's diverse workforce by including all employees in the decision- making process and providing additional education and training for workers to make their fullest contributions may not be enough for Black workers whose primary obstacle to advancing within the workplace is rooted in race and color (Berg, 1984). Due to experiencing years of oppression within corporate America, many Blacks may not be convinced that measures of merely managing diversity will break the elements of racism and oppression in corporate America, which prevents them from moving forward and up the corporate ladder (Berg, 1984).

Under certain conditions of the MEIM scale the interaction of both ethnicity and EID, and its affect on perceived diversity acceptance and leader desirability, may suggest that workers are more aware of the social differences that exist within the workplace and perhaps are expecting leaders to be sensitive to ethnicity and the various stages of EID when attempting to manage diversity. However, these relationships should be retested in future research since changes which increased the reliability of the MEIM reduced the findings to nonsignificant levels.

The MEIM measure created for this study was influenced by Phinney's 1992 MEIM measure. The first fourteen items of Phinney's measure focus on three aspects of ethnic identity:

- positive ethnic attitudes and sense of belonging
- ethnic identity achievement
- ethnic behaviors or practices

For the purpose of this study, the categories remained the same, but the wording of those fourteen items were reworded. In addition, the following items were not used from Phinney's MEIM measure due to their irrelevant areas of focus

- items fifteen through twenty focus on other group orientation
- items twenty-two and twenty-three focus on parent's ethnicity

This may have weakened the ethnic identity measure and resulted in

58

low scale reliability. The administration of the survey may have also affected the respondents.

The word "ethnic," which is cited within most of the scale items, could have lead to a variety of interpretations for White respondents. Many White Americans do not classify themselves as Whites, but as Americans of various European descents. Indeed, Alderfer suggests that American Whites often have difficulty identifying their ethnicity at all (Alderfer, 1982). Such ambiguity within the MEIM may have attributed to the low reliability of the scale. Future research with the MEIM may need to aid White respondents in determining the "ethnicity" about which they are being surveyed.

In this study, respondents were asked to think about their own ethnicity and EID before reading and evaluating the three scenarios. However, having the respondents think about their own ethnicity and EID may have persuaded the respondents to respond in a socially desirable manner when evaluating the three scenarios.

Thomas' argument was that workers are more likely to make full contributions if leaders are accepting of diversity than if leaders are nonaccepting of diversity (Thomas, 1996). This lead to the prediction in this study that leaders who are perceived as having a high level of acceptance of diversity will be judged as better to work for than leaders who are perceived as having lower level of acceptance of diversity. Results supported this prediction. Thus, in looking at the differences between perceived acceptance and desirability scores among respondents, those who rated a leader high on diversity acceptance also rated the leader high on desirability. This trend may indicate that depending on how the leader addresses diversity issues the work relationship between worker and leader is affected. Thomas may be right that diversity acceptance by leaders is an expected and important part of modern organizational life.

Although this study was not successful in finding a relationship between EID and its effect on perceived diversity acceptance and desirability to work for leaders, the results do suggest that diversity acceptance by leaders is important to workers. Further, Thomas' theoretical work and categories are supported by these findings. These findings may imply that one's ethnicity and EID are no longer the key determinants used for working through diversity issues.

Suggestions for Future Research

This study could be enhanced by exploring perceptions of diversity acceptance and leader desirability for among a greater number of workers belonging to other racial groups in industries other than retail. Such additional information will undoubtedly strengthen the general conclusions of this study.

For the purpose of this study, Phinney's 1992 MEIM measure was modified. Thus, the three sub- scales, affirmation and belonging, ethnic identity achievement, and ethnic behaviors and practices, could be used in full in future studies.

In this study the reliability for the MEIM scale was 58 percent. Thus, a post-hoc test was conducted on the MEIM scale to further investigate the items on the MEIM scale which contributed to the statistical insignificance of Hypothesis 3, and the significance of Hypotheses 4a and 4b. As a result of running an inter-item correlation, items 7, 8, and 10 were taken out of the scale due to their low mean scores as compared to the other 11 items on the scale. The weakness within these items may be due to their negative wording. In reading items 7, 8, and 10, respondents may have responded to them as if they were positive items, thus confusing the respondents. Once the items were omitted a reliability analysis was performed on the MEIM scale. Interestingly enough, the reliability of the scale increased to 73 percent. With such an increase in the reliability level, Hypotheses 3 and 4 were also retested to see if the revised scale would create a difference in their statistical significance. Hypothesis 3 remained statistically insignificant; however, Hypotheses 4a and 4b changed from statistically significant to insignificant.

Such a change in the statistical significance of Hypothesis 4 may be indicative of the importance of items 7, 8, and 10 and that perhaps these three items should be reworded and remain in the MEIM scale to further investigate the interaction of ethnicity and ethnic identity development and its affect on perceived diversity acceptance of leader and perceived desirability of leader. In addition, the reliability of the survey may be strengthened by reversing the order of the two instruments (MEIM measure and three scenario survey), reliability of MEIM scales was 58 percent and reliability of the workers' perception scale was 71 percent.

Results of Hypothesis 5 indicate that diversity acceptance and desirability to work for leader scores were so highly correlated that respondents may have failed to distinguish the two concepts. Thus future research should investigate this relationship to determine any systematic confounding.

The above findings suggest that ethnic identity development and ethnicity, when explored together, do affect the perceptions of White and Black workers in defining "diversity" and their desire to work for a leader whom they believe has accepted diversity and is effective in resolving diversity issues within the workplace. It is also apparent within this study that there is a trend among White and Black workers to desire a leader, regardless of the leader's ethnicity, that seeks to change aspects of an organization's structure which prevent all employees from fully contributing and achieving their career goals. The finding that there is a greater desire to work for Scenario Three leader (managing diversity) than Scenario One leader (Affirmative Action) and Scenario Two leader (valuing differences) indicates that White and Black workers are not necessarily convinced that past ways of managing diversity are effective in resolving their diverse issues.

Backlash to Affirmative Action may mean that Scenario One (Affirmative Action) and Scenario Two (valuing differences) leaders are perceived quite differently from one another. Based on Thomas' (1991) assumptions in 1991, this study pooled Scenarios One and Two. However, in efforts to further investigate this trend, further testing should be conducted on Hypotheses 1a and 1b, testing Scenario One and Scenario Two leaders separately in comparison to Scenario Three leaders. Such additional information may shed light on how Black and White workers perceive the ineffectiveness of both Affirmative Action and valuing differences approaches. Today, it may be true that White and Black workers believe that leaders have accepted diversity if they take measures to include all employees in the decision-making process and provide opportunities for all employees to fully contribute within the organization.

Part Two

Women Leaders: Perception of Deviance within the Workplace

The present study elaborates on the phenomenon of in-group bias (Marques, Yzerbt, and Leyens, 1988) and social power within White Corporate America. The phenomenon, coined the "black sheep effect," is viewed as the salient behaviors of in-group members, as compared to that of out-group members, that can affect the subjects' social identity (Marques, Yzerbt, and Leyens, 1988). It is being predicted, based on the black sheep effect, that judgments about both likable and unlikable in-group members are more extreme than judgments about out-group members (Marques, Yzerbt, and Leyens, 1988). And, it is also being predicted, based on the social power theory, that people form social perceptions merely on the basis of frequency information (Lord and Alliger, 1985).

Thus it is being predicted that:

- Black women in a leadership role will experience more deviant behavior from their subordinates than White women in leadership roles
- Black women in a leadership role will judge their Black subordinates' acts of deviance to be more severe than their White subordinates' acts of deviance
- White women in a leadership role will judge their Black subordinates' acts of deviance to be more severe than their White subordinates' acts of deviance

Chapter VI
Introduction

As the Workforce 2000 continues to diversify itself with respect to gender and race (Sekaran and Leong, 1992), the relationship between leader and subordinate has a great deal of influence on how both the leader and subordinate perceive one another's behavior within the organization. Since women represent the largest growth sector and Hispanics and Blacks are the fastest growing Minority groups, it stands to reason that these populations will demand the most attention (Sekaran and Leong, 1992).

Within the context of leadership perception, relationships among Black women and White women leaders will require more attention as previously ignored issues of difference surface (Sekaran and Leong, 1992). Working-class women, and women of color in particular, confront sexist oppression in a way that reflects the real and complex objective interconnections between economic, racial, and sexual oppression (Davis, 1989) whereas a White middle-class woman's experience of sexism incorporates a relatively isolated form of this oppression (Davis, 1989). Working-class women's experiences necessarily place sexism in its context of class exploitation and Black women's experiences further integrate gender oppression within the realities of racism (Davis, 1989; Giddings, 1984; Lerner, 1973).

According to Alderfer, racism, unlike all of the other isms, is complex in that the concept provides insight into America's ongoing race relations between Blacks and Whites (Alderfer, 1982). Exploitation of Blacks by Whites has existed in the territory of the United States since before the country's founding. Although slavery has been abolished for more than a hundred years, patterns of economic and social discrimination against Blacks in predominantly White organizations continue to exist to this day.

In light of the Black and White race relations in America, Black and White female managers in White corporate America will bring their own unique set of experiences to the work environment. When White female managers speak of being oppressed within White corporate America it is safe to assume that they are strictly speaking of differential treatment that is rooted in sexism (Alderfer, 1982; Sekaran and Leong, 1992). However, when Black women managers speak of oppression within White corporate America it is not safe to assume that they are just speaking of differential treatment that is rooted in gender.

Given that White corporate America is dominated by White males, it would be safe to assume that Black female managers experience racial oppression first before sexism (Campbell, 1994; Alderfer, 1982; McIntosh, 1988). These different experiences that Black and White female managers bring to the workplace greatly influence how they will interact with their subordinates.

The purpose of this study is to better understand the categorical process in which a leader classifies deviant behavior among her subordinates. Taking into consideration the increased number of female leaders and Minority subordinates within White corporate America, the focus of this study will be on the relationship between Black and White female leaders and their Black and White subordinates.

Although women leaders (Black and White) and their Black and White subordinates represent "Minority" groups within White corporate America, it is the practice of sexism within the context of racism that may differentiate the perceptions of the Black female leader from those of White female leaders (Sekaran, and Leong, 1992). The differential relationships that exist between women leaders (Black and White) and their Black and White subordinates can be understood by considering perceptions that are rooted within in-group experiences. Within the field of psychology, extensive research has been conducted in the areas of inter-group and intra-group dynamics; specifically in-group bias (Marques, Robalo, and Rocha, 1992), "black sheep" effect (Marques and Yzerbt, 1988; Marques, Yzerbt, and Leyens, 1988), and social power (Tajfel, 1982).

Chapter VII
Review of the Literature

Stereotyping and Inter-group Perceptions

The whole notion of stereotypes holds such tremendous weight in our society. Although there are both positive and negative stereotypes, groups tend to make use of the negative stereotypes when there is a need to compete (Berg, 1984).

Objectivity and Prejudice

According to Berg the perspective of inter-group theory suggests that one's group membership is directly linked to the process of making judgments, especially when competition or conflict is involved. Group membership influences both the perception and interpretation of events, and these perceptions and interpretations produce the facts that shape beliefs about groups (Berg, 1984).

> The factual basis for negative attitudes toward groups must be understood as being itself an expression of the inter-group relations. Just as negative attitudes are often a function of internal group dynamics, the facts that underlie beliefs are often a function of inter-group dynamics.

These negative attitudes that are expressed in inter-group relations are no more than stereotypes. Inter-group relations between Whites and Blacks in America is rooted in the perceived notion that one group (Blacks) is a threat to another group's (Whites) social well-being (access to scarce resources). Hence, negative stereotypes have been generated on the premise that there are differences between groups as well as within groups for the sake of possessing or obtaining scarce resources.

67

In-Group Bias and the Black Sheep Effect

The process by which we categorize individuals is based upon their group's identity. The fact that one category includes one's self (in-group) and the other category (out-group) does not have enormous implications for inter-group perception (Rothbart, Dawes, and Park, 1984).

One of the implications examined in the Rothbart and associates 1984 study was that a group will be perceived differently by its own members than by outsiders. As a result of the Rothbart and associates study the following misperceptions were generated in light of differential biases between groups:

- mental representations (stereotypes) of groups determine not only how we perceive out-group members but in-group members as well
- in-group members will exaggerate their opinions of in-group members more than out-group members.

Whether we consider ourselves to belong to the in-group or out-group, our self-identity is attached to that particular group's standards. As group members it is important to us to have a sense of belonging and acceptance. Therefore, if there are any group members around us who behave in such a way that would threaten the integrity of the group's identity, we would have a desire to separate ourselves from those members (Jones, 1986; Marques, Robalo, and Rocha, 1992).

According to Marques and associates in 1992, self-definition becomes attached to norm specifications, defining a positive social identity, and in-group bias emerges from this process, to express a positive orientation toward the social self (in other words, in-group favoritism). However, in-group bias refers to comparisons between the whole in-group and out-group. With the black sheep effect Marques and associates have addressed to situations in which inter-group and intra-group differentiation co-occur. In such situations, subjects upgrade in-group members who bolster normative identity standards, and derogate members who act against such standards, as compared to out-group members.

In this context, judgmental extremity toward in-group members seems to be caused by an underlying attitude of in-group favoritism (Marques, Robalo, and Rocha, 1992). While relative upgrading of likeable in-group members is a straight manifestation of in-group favoritism, downgrading unlikeable ones would be a negative response to threats to social identity coming from inside the in-group (Marques, Robalo, and Rocha, 1992). For example, we acknowledge and support those members that enhance our group identity, and we do not give our support to those members who derogate the identity of the group. In a series of studies conducted by Marques and associates, it was observed that the effects of threat caused in-group members to evaluate likeable and unlikeable members more positively and more negatively than likeable and unlikeable out-group members.

However, in the same way as in-group bias emerges mostly for relevant social identity dimensions, so the black sheep effect was observed only when judgmental dimensions were relevant for subjects' social identity (Marques, Robalo, and Rocha, 1992; Marques and Yzerbt, 1988; Marques, Yzerbt, and Leyens, 1988). While in-group bias becomes apparent when one's social identity becomes threatened by another group member, group members will identify a "black" sheep within the group to explain undesirable group behaviors. This study sheds light on how in-group favoritism can become in-group bias when the social image of a group is threatened by the behavior of an in-group member.

The standards set for desirable and undesirable behaviors within White corporate America reflect the racist ideology of White America (Alderfer, 1982). As the dominant group in America, Whites have managed to oppress other racial groups through acts of racism, all of which are rooted in the ideology that Whites are inherently superior physically, biologically, culturally, and socially (Alderfer, 1982). With respect to this study, Black women managers may be considered to be in a political position of proving themselves to be worthy in the eyes of their White male and female peers within their organization. Thus, corporate America constitutes a condition of threat (Alderfer, 1982; Marques, Robalo, and Rocha, 1992). If this presumption is accurate, this would lead to in-group predictions of Black women leaders expressing that they experience more deviant behavior from their subordinates than White women in leadership roles, and that Black women in leadership roles will judge their Black subordinates' acts of deviance to be more severe than their White subordinates' acts of deviance.

According to Jones, many Black managers feel the social pressure to become more like Whites. This is expressed in the act(s) of devaluing other Blacks, in an effort to get ahead within their organizations. Jones contends that White racism in America has empowered Whites to socially influence other racial groups to become more White in their plight for the scarce resources that Whites possess (Jones, 1986).

Social Power

Social power can best be described as the phenomenon in which a group has more social influence over another group of people in a given society as in the case between White and Black Americans. Whites are viewed to have social power because of the privileges they experience within our society. Regardless of their gender, Whites do not have to compete against one another for the "scarce" resources (for example, money, property . . .) (McIntosh, 1988). On the other hand, Blacks are viewed to be a less influential group in our society because they do not have direct access to the "scarce" resources.

These groups are kept separate as a function of social stereotyping. Black and White women managers compete for the same "scarce" resources, and based on their race they are either denied access or granted privileges within the organization (Alderfer, 1982; Sekaran and Leong, 1992). Aware of one another's position within the organization, Black and White women managers may judge one another based on preexisting social stereotypes, but may also operate off of these ethnic notions when interacting with their subordinates (Rothbart, Dawes, and Park, 1984).

Contact

Integral to the process of self- and social identity in inter-group relations is the notion of contact. Low contact leads to issues of prejudice and discrimination. As in the case of White racism, White Americans have an internal positive picture of Whites and a negative picture of Blacks (Jones, 1986).

According to Aldefer, America's history of White racism has enabled Whites to interact with Blacks as little as possible, hence preventing them from learning in depth about Blacks in general (Aldefer, 1982). The minimal knowledge that Whites do possess about Blacks has been greatly distorted through the use of stereotyping, all in an effort to keep Blacks oppressed. To the contrary, America's White racial history has made it necessary for Blacks and other Minorities to interact with Whites on a daily basis to get their needs met. And, unlike the negative stereotypes that Whites like to promote about other racial groups, the knowledge that Blacks and other racial groups possess about Whites has primarily been that of superiority.

White Privilege

In addition to being members of the "majority" group possessing a great deal of negative knowledge about the "Minority" group, Whites also benefit from numerous societal "privileges" that are not available to Minority group members (McIntosh, 1988). As defined by Sekaran and Leong, privilege can and does coexist with oppression, and being a victim of one form of discrimination does not make one immune to victimizing someone else on a different basis.

> And, if it is understood that to some extent all women are oppressed, to what extent can a woman, or a group of women also act as oppressor should be examined (Sekeran and Leong, 1992).

White privilege has provided White women and men protection of a culture and social norms and values that justify their social power within America. And, not having to define themselves in terms of race, Whites usually do not understand the effects of their "Whiteness" and culture (Sekaran and Leong, 1992; Alderfer, 1982; Campbell, 1994). As the dominant group, White women do not have to work through their own issues of race and racism. If, as asserted by some researchers, as majority group members, White women fail to recognize that they are White, they may then unconditionally support the White male system (Sekaran and Leong, 1992; Alderfer, 1982; McIntosh, 1988). While a White woman's gender creates differences, her race assumes a privilege of assimilation into predominantly White male organizations that women of color do not have (Sekaran and Leong, 1992; Alderfer, 1982; Campbell, 1994).

McIntosh contends that White privilege is a condition that affects the daily lives of Whites and establishes their social identity among themselves and with other ethnic groups (McIntosh, 1988). Through their status of power and privilege Whites can be assured higher education, preferred housing, career opportunities, and a life not affected by racism nor discrimination (McIntosh, 1988). In her extensive write-up on White privilege, McIntosh lists 46 conditions of daily experiences which benefit Whites. Among those conditions are the following privileges of Whites in the U.S.:

- They can avoid spending time with Blacks
- They are guaranteed to live in any area they can afford and or want
- They are guaranteed to see positive images of themselves in the media
- They are taught that their race group made America History what it is
- They are guaranteed educational rights without facing discrimination
- They are allowed to ignore the plight of people of color

For these reasons, Black women and White women need to explore the assumptions that they bring to their work relationships (Sekaran and Leong, 1992). Given that this is not an easy nor fast process, some authors argue that this dialogue must come from the dominant group with its privileged power base and status; hence, White women must take a lead in initiating the dialogue (Sekaran, and Leong, 1992; Alderfer, 1982). These same authors contend that White women have traditionally assumed little responsibility for understanding racism and have re-enforced White racism by failing to identify with the White race and its historical racism. Thus, theories of social power and White privilege would lead to a prediction within this study that White women in leadership roles will judge their Black subordinates' acts of deviance to be more severe than their White subordinates' acts of deviance.

Black Women Leaders in White Corporate America

Black women leaders within the workforce represent a group of women who experience triple oppression: a) gender, b) race, and c) class (Davis, 1983). Unlike many of their foremothers, whose space within the workforce resembled slave duties (caretakers, housekeepers, cooks, nursemaids), Black women are progressively moving up within the structure of White corporate America (Campbell, 1994). Today's "new" Black woman is devoted to spending a tremendous amount of time and energy to establish her professional identity (Bell, 1990). However, as professionals

Black women are faced with the dual challenge of transforming stereotypical images and simultaneously creating new professional roles (Campbell, 1994; Bell, 1990; Allen, 1979).

Black women leaders have found themselves confronted with two key issues within the workplace: a) in-group conflict, and b) maintaining a "positive" social identity (Marques, Robalo, and Rocha, 1992). Contrary to the perceived view that Black women leaders tend to give loyalty to race first (Bell, 1992), as an in-group member Black women leaders would expect to have their leadership role taken for granted by their Black subordinates (Campbell, 1994).

Given that their position of power is unique in that their ethnicity is the same as their Black female leader, Black subordinates would seek preferential treatment from their Black female leader. Hence, Black women leaders would expect their Black subordinates to break the cultural rules of the organization more frequently than their White subordinates (Campbell, 1994). In addition to maintaining their subordinates' behavior, Black women leaders have found themselves protecting their acquired "positive" social image (Campbell, 1994). This need of wanting to protect their acquired "positive" social image is rooted in the fear of not wanting to reflect any of the negative images about Blacks that are communicated within the dominant group (Campbell, 1994; Bell, 1990). Thus, the theory on the "new" Black woman leads to a prediction within this study that Black women in leadership roles will judge their Black subordinates' acts of deviance to be more severe than their White subordinates' acts of deviance.

White Women Leaders in White Corporate America

In general, people feel most comfortable both personally and professionally with those whom they are most like (Sekaran and Leong, 1992). Thus, Black women have been made to feel uncomfortable with respect and gender in work environments that are dominated by Whites (Sekaran and Leong, 1992). On the other hand, the social political status of White women within White corporate America allows them to identify more with White male values and assimilate more easily and distinctively with both their race and gender within the work environment than their Black counterparts (Sekaran and Leong, 1992).

White women leaders within the workforce represent a group of women who experience double oppression: a) gender, and b) class (Davis,

73

1983; Sekaran and Leong, 1992). And, unlike many of their foremothers, White women leaders have found self-worth outside of their household duties of wife and mother (Bell, 1990; Campbell, 1994; Davis, 1983). Although White women leaders have experienced much hardship in obtaining their rightful place within White corporate America, their inheritance of White social power has softened the blows of their plight (McIntosh, 1988). Given racial privilege in majority White organizations, White women leaders are readily accepted and or privileged to be apart of "the club" (Sekaran and Leong, 1992).

Sekaran and Leong contend that the position of White women leaders in an organization is affected by ways in which decision makers choose to assign limited opportunities among women and Minorities. Due to their unique position within the workforce, White women leaders have found themselves confronted with two key issues: a) out-group conflict, and b) maintaining a "positive" social identity (Marques, Robalo, and Rocha, 1992). As out-group members White women leaders would expect their Black subordinates to be noncompliant. This may be due to the lack of power Black subordinates possess in their work relationship with a White woman leader, thus, influencing them to seek power through such deviant behaviors as distrust, suspicion, passive-aggression, and manipulation (Penderhughes, 1989). In addition to maintaining the behavior of their subordinates, White women leaders are under the pressure of proving themselves to be socially acceptable by disproving any negative stereotypes that White males possess about gender differences.

Hypothesis 1

Black women in a leadership role will experience more deviant behavior from their subordinates than White women in leadership roles. This prediction is supported by research that explores perceptual influences of social power. Black women leaders will assume that their relative lower social power will relate to their subordinates' lack of power within the organization; therefore, they will perceive greater deviance than White women leaders.

Hypothesis 2

Black women in a leadership role will judge their Black subordinates' acts of deviance to be more severe than their White subordinates' acts of deviance. Based on the black sheep effect literature, Black women leaders within White corporate America hold a unique position with respect to race and gender. Thus, Black women leaders' in-group identity with their Black subordinates will cause them to be more judgmental of their Black subordinates' behavior than their White subordinates' behavior.

Hypothesis 3

White women in a leadership role will judge their Black subordinates' acts of deviance to be more severe than their White subordinates' acts of deviance. This prediction is supported by studies on White privilege and in-group/out-group exposure.

Given that White women leaders hold a unique position within White corporate America with respect to race and gender, White women leaders will have had less exposure to Blacks than to Whites. Thus, this low out-group familiarity with their Black subordinates will cause them to be more judgmental of their Black subordinates' behavior than their White subordinates' behavior.

Chapter VIII
Methods

Participants

An exploratory survey was conducted to measure perceptions of deviance within the workplace among White and Black female leaders. Ten Black women and ten White women leaders within the retail industry served as voluntary participants. Leadership status was based on the positions of Manager or Assistant Manager. Each leader was required to evaluate ten of their subordinates' acts of deviance. Volunteers were not paid for their participation.

Material

The process of generating an instrument that would effectively measure acts of deviance consisted of randomly asking corporate workers what they perceived as acts of deviance within their respective organizations. Once all desired items were collected, a two-part questionnaire was put together (pre-test and post-test). The two part questionnaire was conducted over the telephone to collect the desired data. Each questionnaire contained two sections: 1) demographics, and 2) acts of deviance. The demographic section contained four items (race, sex, number of years with organization, and title of position) by which to identify the female leaders. The acts of deviance section consisted of ten specific examples of possible subordinate deviant behaviors with a *yes, no,* or *depends* response. At the end of the questionnaire there was an open-ended question of "Can you provide additional acts of deviance?"

Part two of the questionnaire was a performance evaluation of the subordinates' behaviors. Leaders were asked to rate ten subordinates one at a time on their acts of deviance. The same four demographic items used in part one were used here to identify each subordinate. To assess deviance, the same ten questions asked in part one and the additional items provided from the open-ended question were asked in the form of a Likert scale from 1 to 7 (7 being what is considered to be highly deviant).

Procedure

The two-part questionnaire was conducted via telephone, with three White and three Black women leaders. This was done to ensure that all possible deviant behaviors were recognized on part two of the questionnaire, while part one of the questionnaire served as a pre-test to collect additional acts of deviance within the industry. Six (three Black women leaders and three White women leaders) of the twenty participants participated in part one of the two-part questionnaire. All six participants were informed that the purpose of this study was to obtain a better understanding of women leaders' perception of deviance among their subordinates' deviance.

Before reading the questionnaire items to each subject, the participants were asked to identify themselves by their race, number of years with the organization, and title of position (manager or assistant manager). For all six participants all ten items were read from the questionnaire and each participant was given ample time to respond to each item with either a *yes, no,* or *depends* response. Once all ten items were answered, each participant was encouraged to provide additional behaviors of deviance that occur within their workplace. From this process two additional items were collected for part two of the questionnaire.

For part two of the questionnaire all twenty participants participated. Each participant was instructed to select ten of their subordinates whom they believe to have exemplified low or high acts of deviance within the workplace. The participants were advised to randomly choose their ten subordinates to ensure a balance between race, sex, number of years with the organization, and title of position (sales associate or lead associate). Once the participants had selected ten of their subordinates, they were asked to identify each subordinate by race, sex, number of years with organization, and title of position. The participants were advised that they would be evaluating their subordinates' acts of deviance by rating the questions on the questionnaire on a 7-point Likert scale. All twelve items were read from the questionnaire to each participant for each of the ten subordinates.

Chapter IX
Results

Hypothesis 1

The results revealed a slight difference in the amount of deviant behaviors that Black and White women leaders express experiencing from their subordinates. Using an ANOVA (see Table 9.1), Black women leaders have a mean score of 2.42 in comparison to the White women leaders' mean score of 2.22. Although both groups express slight deviant behaviors, the Black women leaders' score revealed they perceived a higher frequency of deviant behaviors than the White women leaders. However, the difference was found to be statistically insignificant (p .05). Thus, while the scores are consistent with Hypothesis 1, it cannot be statistically supported.

Hypothesis 2

The results revealed a slight difference in the amount of deviant behaviors that Black women leaders reported from their Black subordinates when compared to their White subordinates. Using an ANOVA (see Table 9.2), Black subordinates have a mean score of 2.77 in comparison to the White subordinates' mean score of 1.99. Again, the level of deviance perceived for groups slightly varies. However, the Black women leaders' score revealed they are more judgmental of their Black subordinates' behaviors than White women leaders. This difference was found to be statistically significant (p .05). Thus, the scores statistically support Hypothesis 2.

Table 9.1

ANOVA for Hypothesis 1: Black women in leadership roles will experience more deviant behavior than White women in leadership roles.

Ethnic group of leaders	Mean	Std. Dev.	Sum of Square	df	Mean Square	F.	Sig.
Black	2.42	.326					
White	2.22	.609					
Main effects (Ethnic Group)			.204	1	.204	.852	.367

Table 9.2

ANOVA for Hypothesis 2: Black women in leadership roles will judge their Black subordinates' acts of deviance to be more severe than their White subordinates' acts of deviance.

Ethnic group of Subordinates	Mean	Std. Dev.	Sum of Square	df	Mean Square	F.	Sig.
Black	2.77	.545					
White	1.99	.307					
Main effects (Ethnic Group)			3.09	1	3.09	15.78	.000

Hypothesis 3

The results revealed a slight difference in the amount of deviant behaviors that White women leaders experienced from their Black subordinates when compared to their White subordinates. Using an ANOVA (see Table 9.3), White subordinates have a mean score of 2.34 in comparison to the Black subordinates' mean score of 2.26. Although both groups were reported to have few deviant behaviors, the White women leaders' score revealed they perceived a higher frequency of deviant behaviors from White subordinates than from Black subordinates. However, the difference was found to be not statistically significant ($p<.05$). Thus, the scores are not consistent with Hypothesis 3 and are not statistically significant.

Table 9.3

ANOVA for Hypothesis 3: White women in leadership roles will judge their Black subordinates' acts of deviance to be more severe than their White subordinates' acts of deviance.

	Mean	Std. Dev.	Sum of Square	df	Mean Square	F.	Sig.
Ethnic group of Subordinates							
Black	2.34	.631					
White	2.26	1.10					
Main effects (Ethnic Group)			.019	1	.019	.023	.881

Chapter X
Discussion

Within this study three assumptions were made:

1. Women leaders who are perceived to have low social power will express experiencing more deviant behavior from their subordinates than women leaders who are perceived to have high social power.
2. Women leaders who share the same group identity as their subordinates will be more judgmental of in-group acts of deviance than those acts of deviance belonging to the out-group.
3. Women leaders who have low out-group familiarity of their subordinates will be more judgmental of out-group acts of deviance than those acts of deviance belonging to the in-group.

In Hypothesis 1 the findings were statistically insignificant. The findings suggest that the deviant behaviors that Black women leaders express experiencing from their Black and White subordinates may be rooted in inter-group dynamics other than social power. In Hypothesis 3 the findings were not statistically significant, but do not suggest that low out-group familiarity will cause White women leaders to be more judgmental of their Black subordinates' acts of deviance than their White subordinates' acts of deviance. In fact the findings show that where there is low out-group familiarity White women leaders are more judgmental of their White subordinates' acts of deviance than their Black subordinates' acts of deviance. Again, the acts of deviance that White women leaders perceive in White subordinates maybe rooted in intra-group dynamics other than low out-group familiarity. Maybe White women leaders are perceived to have low social power among their White subordinates, as Black women leaders are perceived to have low social power among their Black subordinates.

In Hypothesis 2 the findings were statistically significant. Black women leaders are more judgmental of the acts of deviance by their Black subordinates than they are of their White subordinates. The findings from Hypothesis 2 suggest that Black women leaders are concerned about protecting their "positive" identity; thus, they are socially motivated to separate themselves from in-group members that display undesirable behaviors in White organizations.

Suggestions for Future Research

Although Hypothesis 2 was significant, this study does not go without its limitations. Given that this study was conducted for exploratory purposes only, the use of controls was absent. There were no control groups (other racial groups) to test against the tested groups (Black and White women leaders and their Black and White subordinates). The two-part questionnaire used in collecting the data was culturally biased. All of the items on the questionnaire were chosen to represent behaviors that went against the standards within White corporate culture. Furthermore, the sample size was quite small (twenty participants—ten of each Black and White women leaders), and the participants reported their perceptions of deviance among their subordinates (two hundred informal evaluations total). There was no actual collection of performance evaluations of subordinates.

To enhance this study, the instrument used to collect the desired data should also include a qualitative component. The use of interviews may elicit data that is not culturally biased. The sample size may or may not be enlarged depending on the length of the interviews. In addition to interviewing Black and White women leaders about their perceptions of deviance among their Black and White subordinates, the study should also include several interviews from women leaders of other racial groups regarding their perceptions of deviance within the workplace. And, if possible, formal evaluation reports of subordinates should be collected and analyzed.

Appendixes

WORKERS' PERCEPTION OF LEADERS' DIVERSITY ACCEPTANCE SURVEY

(FORM A)

A. Background. Please provide the information below, by circling the appropriate category for each demographic category (ethnicity, gender, age and years with organization).

Ethnicity	Gender	Age	Years with organization	Title of Position
American Indian	Female	26 to 35	1 to 5 years	Manager
Black, non-Hispanic	Male	18 to 25	Less than 1 year	Assistant Manager
Asian or Pacific Islander		36 to 45	5 to 10 years	Sales Associate
Hispanic		46 plus	More than 10 years	
White, non-Hispanic				

B. Use the scale below to indicate how much you agree or disagree with each statement.

4: Strongly agree	3: Somewhat agree	2: Somewhat disagree	1: Strongly disagree

1. I have spent time trying to find out about my ethnic culture. _____
2. I am active in organizations or groups that include mostly members of my ethnic group. _____
3. I have a clear sense of my ethnic background and what it means to me. _____
4. I like getting to know people from other ethnic groups. _____
5. I think a lot about how my life is affected by my ethnic group membership. _____
6. I am happy that I belong to my ethnic group. _____
7. I sometimes feel that different ethnic groups should not mix together. _____
8. I am not really clear about the role of my ethnicity in my life. _____
9. I often spend time with members from other ethnic groups. _____
10. I really haven't spent much time learning about my ethnic cultural background. _____
11. I have a strong sense of belonging to my ethnic group. _____
12. I somewhat understand what my ethnic group means to me in terms of relating to my own group members and other group members. _____
13. I often speak with others to learn more about my ethnic background. _____
14. I am proud of my ethnic group and its accomplishments. _____

C. Perceptions of Diversity Acceptance. Using the scenarios below, please indicate to which extent you believe the manager has accepted diversity, and how desirable the manager is to work for.

Scenario One. Statement of a White leader
    With the increased emphasis being placed on diversity awareness within the workplace, I remain active in the area of recruiting more Minority and Women workers at entry level positions. With greater numbers of Minorities and Women workers within our organization we will successfully address diversity. I think this is the right approach in dealing with diversity issues within the workplace.
    As a White leader I am aware of the demands placed on Minority and Women workers to enter into corporate culture. Therefore, I am involved in the recruitment of Women and Minorities.

Perception of Leaders' Diversity Acceptance Scale

1. Acceptance of Diversity

1	2	3	4	5	6	7
non-accepting						accepting

2. Desirable to work for

1	2	3	4	5	6	7
undesirable						desirable

Scenario Two. Statement of a Black leader
    The demographics of today's workforce are rapidly changing: older workforce, more Women and Minority workers, more Immigrant workers, and an increased gap of uneducated and educated workers. With such a diverse workforce to manage, I am busy with ensuring that single parents are allowed flex-time (if the job allows), keeping a visual calendar of all ethnic holidays and celebrations, and posting all relevant training that will improve communication skills and awareness of how to appreciate our differences. I think we are taking the right approach to diversity this way.
    As a Black leader I like to acknowledge my workers' differences and similarities and find it necessary to encourage all of my workers to attend the appropriate training sessions that are available, as well as observe ethnic holidays/celebrations.

1. Acceptance of Diversity

1	2	3	4	5	6	7
non-accepting						accepting

2. Desirable to work for

1	2	3	4	5	6	7
undesirable						desirable

Scenario Three. Statement of a White leader

     Diversity within the work place not only acknowledges gender and race, but lifestyle, education, and occupational skills. To manage such a complex workforce is more demanding these days. Minority and Women workers are entering the workplace with more confidence of being who they are. As a manager, I am interested in my workers' diverse needs, and have encouraged my organization to conduct worker opinion surveys. As we move toward the Twenty-first century, managers are going to have to hear the "voice" of their employees if they are to tap into the full potential of the organizations' "human resources." We will also need to be sure that our decision teams are inclusive of our diversity. I think we are taking the right approach to diversity this way.

     As a White leader I find it necessary to work with my workers and to make every effort possible to ensure that the organization meets their work needs and includes them in decision making.

1. Acceptance of Diversity

| 1 | 2 | 3 | 4 | 5 | 6 | 7 |
| non-accepting | | | | | | accepting |

2. Desirable to work for

| 1 | 2 | 3 | 4 | 5 | 6 | 7 |
| undesirable | | | | | | desirable |

WORKERS' PERCEPTION OF LEADERS' DIVERSITY ACCEPTANCE SURVEY

(FORM B)

A. Background. Please provide the information below, by circling the appropriate   category for each demographic category (ethnicity, gender, age and years with organization).

Ethnicity	Gender	Age	Years with organization	Title of Position
American Indian	Female	26 to 35	1 to 5 years	Manager
Black, non-Hispanic	Male	18 to 25	Less than 1 year	Assistant Manager
Asian or Pacific Islander		36 to 45	5 to 10 years	Sales Associate
Hispanic		46 plus	More than 10 years	
White, non-Hispanic				

B. Use the scale below to indicate how much you agree or disagree with each statement.

4: Strongly agree	3: Somewhat agree	2: Somewhat disagree	1: Strongly disagree

1. I have spent time trying to find out about my ethnic culture. _____
2. I am active in organizations or groups that include mostly members of my ethnic group. _____
3. I have a clear sense of my ethnic background and what it means to me. _____
4. I like getting to know people from other ethnic groups. _____
5. I think a lot about how my life is affected by my ethnic group membership. _____
6. I am happy that I belong to my ethnic group. _____
7. I sometimes feel that different ethnic groups should not mix together. _____
8. I am not really clear about the role of my ethnicity in my life. _____
9. I often spend time with members from other ethnic groups. _____
10. I really haven't spent much time learning about my ethnic cultural background. _____
11. I have a strong sense of belonging to my ethnic group. _____
12. I somewhat understand what my ethnic group means to me in terms of relating to my own group members and other group members. _____
13. I often speak with others to learn more about my ethnic background. _____
14. I am proud of my ethnic group and its accomplishments. _____

90

C. Perceptions of Diversity Acceptance. Using the scenarios below, please indicate to which extent you believe the manager has accepted diversity, and how desirable the manager is to work for.

Scenario One. Statement of a Black leader
    With the increased emphasis being placed on diversity awareness within the workplace, I remain active in the area of recruiting more Minority and Women workers at entry level positions. With greater numbers of Minorities and Women workers within our organization we will successfully address diversity. I think this is the right approach in dealing with diversity issues within the workplace.
    As a Black leader I am aware of the demands placed on Minority and Women workers to enter into corporate culture. Therefore, I am involved in the recruitment of Women and Minorities.

Perception of Leaders' Diversity Acceptance Scale

1. Acceptance of Diversity

1	2	3	4	5	6	7
non-accepting						accepting

2. Desirable to work for

1	2	3	4	5	6	7
undesirable						desirable

Scenario Two. Statement of a White leader
    The demographics of today's workforce are rapidly changing: older workforce, more Women and Minority workers, more Immigrant workers, and an increased gap of uneducated and educated workers. With such a diverse workforce to manage, I am busy with ensuring that single parents are allowed flex-time (if the job allows), keeping a visual calendar of all ethnic holidays and celebrations, and posting all relevant training that will improve communication skills and awareness of how to appreciate our differences. I think we are taking the right approach to diversity this way.
    As a White leader I like to acknowledge my workers' differences and similarities and find it necessary to encourage all of my workers to attend the appropriate training sessions that are available, as well as observe ethnic holidays/celebrations.

Perception of Leaders' Diversity Acceptance Scale

1. Acceptance of Diversity

1	2	3	4	5	6	7
non-accepting						accepting

2. Desirable to work for

1	2	3	4	5	6	7
undesirable						desirable

Scenario Three. Statement of a Black leader

Diversity within the work place not only acknowledges gender and race, but lifestyle, education, and occupational skills. To manage such a complex workforce is more demanding these days. Minority and Women workers are entering the workplace with more confidence of being who they are. As a manager, I am interested in my workers' diverse needs, and have encouraged my organization to conduct worker opinion surveys. As we move toward the Twenty-first century, managers are going to have to hear the "voice" of their employees if they are to tap into the full potential of the organizations' "human resources." We will also need to be sure that our decision teams are inclusive of our diversity. I think we are taking the right approach to diversity this way.

As a Black leader I find it necessary to work with my workers and to make every effort possible to ensure that the organization meets their work needs and includes them in decision making.

Perception of Leaders' Diversity Acceptance Scale

1. Acceptance of Diversity

1	2	3	4	5	6	7
non-accepting						accepting

2. Desirable to work for

1	2	3	4	5	6	7
undesirable						desirable

Appendix C

Research Questionnaire: Leaders' Perception of Deviance (Form A)

A. Background. Please provide the information below.

  1. Race_____
  2. Sex_____
  3. Number of years with organization_____
  4. Title position within the organization_____

B. Perceptions of deviance. Using the questions below, please indicate to which extent you believe a subordinate's behavior to be deviant.

1. When a subordinate takes an extended lunch or dinner break beyond prescribed time limit, is that an act of deviance?

Yes No Depends

2. When a subordinate arrives more than five minutes late to work, is that an act of deviance?

Yes No Depends

3. When a subordinate leaves work more than five minutes early, is that an act of deviance?

Yes No Depends

4. When a subordinate takes more than allowed breaks, is that an act of deviance?

Yes No Depends

5. When a subordinate modifies his or her work assignments to meet his or her needs, is that an act of deviance?

Yes No Depends

6. When a subordinate takes the authority to delegate his or her work duties to co-workers, is that an act of deviance?

Yes No Depends

7. When a subordinate utilizes the office phone to make personal calls, is that an act of deviance?

Yes No Depends

8. When a subordinate dresses outside of the dress code, is that an act of deviance?

        Yes   No   Depends

9. When a subordinate engages in casual conversations with other co-workers while working, is that an act of deviance?

        Yes   No   Depends

10. When a subordinate eats within the work area, is that an act of deviance?

        Yes   No   Depends

C. Please use the space below to provide further examples of deviant behaviors that are exemplified by your subordinates.

_____

_____

_____

Appendix D

Evaluating Subordinates' acts of Deviance Questionnaire (Form B)

A. Background of leader. Please provide the information below.

  1. Race_____
  2. Sex_____
  3. Number of years with organization_____
  4. Title position within the organization_____

  B. Background of subordinate. Please provide the information below.

  1. Race_____
  2. Sex_____
  3. Number of years with organization_____
  4. Title position within the organization_____

C. Acts of deviance rating scale

  1. Subordinate takes an extended lunch or dinner break beyond prescribed time
     limit

     1   2   3   4   5   6   7
     not deviant   deviant

  2. Subordinate arrives more than five minutes late to work

     1   2   3   4   5   6   7
     not deviant   deviant

  3. Subordinate leaves work more than five minutes early

     1   2   3   4   5   6   7
     not deviant   deviant

  4. Subordinate takes more than allowed breaks

     1   2   3   4   5   6   7
     not deviant   deviant

  5. Subordinate modifies his or her work assignment to meet his or her needs

     1   2   3   4   5   6   7
     not deviant   deviant

6. Subordinate takes the authority to delegate his or her work duties to co-workers

| 1 | 2 | 3 | 4 | 5 | 6 | 7 |
| not deviant | | | | | | deviant |

7. Subordinate utilizes the office phone to make personal calls

| 1 | 2 | 3 | 4 | 5 | 6 | 7 |
| not deviant | | | | | | deviant |

8. Subordinate dresses outside of the dress code

| 1 | 2 | 3 | 4 | 5 | 6 | 7 |
| not deviant | | | | | | deviant |

9. Subordinate engages in casual conversations with other co-workers while working

| 1 | 2 | 3 | 4 | 5 | 6 | 7 |
| not deviant | | | | | | deviant |

10. Subordinate eats within the work area

| 1 | 2 | 3 | 4 | 5 | 6 | 7 |
| not deviant | | | | | | deviant |

11. Subordinate alters time card to meet his or her needs

| 1 | 2 | 3 | 4 | 5 | 6 | 7 |
| not deviant | | | | | | deviant |

12. Subordinate arrives to work and is not prepared to work

| 1 | 2 | 3 | 4 | 5 | 6 | 7 |
| not deviant | | | | | | deviant |

References

Alderfer, C.P. (1982). "Problems of Changing White Males' Behavior and Beliefs Concerning Race Relations," in *Change in Organizations.* (pp. 122–165). San Francisco: Jossey-Bass Publishers.

Allen, W. R. (1979, Summer). "Family Roles, Occupational Statuses, and Achievement Orientations among Black Women in the United States," in *Signs.* Four, (4), (pp. 670–686).

Allport, G. (1979). *The Nature of Prejudice.* Addison-Wesley Publishing Company.

Banton, M. (1987). *Racial Theories.* Cambridge, MA: Cambridge University Press.

Bell, D. (1996). "Racism Is the Cause of Problems for Blacks," in D. Bender and B. Leone (Eds.) *Race Relations: Opposing Viewpoints.* (pp. 17–23), San Diego, CA: Greenhaven Press, Inc.

Bell, E. L. (1990). "The Bicultural Life Experience of Career-Oriented Black Women," in *Journal of Organizational Behavior,* Eleven, (pp. 459–477).

Bell, E. L. (1992, September). "Myths, Stereotypes, and Realities of Black Women: A Personal Reflection," *The Journal of Applied Behavioral Science, Twenty-eight,* (3), (pp. 363–376).

Berg, D. N. (1984, January/February). "Objectivity and Prejudice," in *American Behavioral Scientist,* Twenty-seven, (3), (pp. 387–402).

Blauner, R. (1992). "The Ambiguities of Racial Change," in M. L. Anderson and P. H. Collins, *Race, Class, and Gender.* (pp. 54–65), Cambridge University Press.

Block, C. J., Roberson, L. A., and Neuger, D. A. (1992). "Racial Identity Theory: A framework for understanding attitudes toward workforce diversity," essay presented at the Society for Industrial Organizational Psychology Convention, April 1992, San Francisco, CA.

Bonacich, E. (1992). "Inequality in America: The Failure of the American System for People of Color," in M. L. Anderson and P. H. Collins, *Race, Class, and Gender.* (pp. 96–110), Cambridge University Press.

Bromely, D. G., and Longino, C. F., Jr. (1972). *White Racism and Black Americans.* Cambridge, MA.

Campbell, B. M. (1994). *Brothers and Sisters.* New York: G. P. Putnam's Sons.

Clark, K. B. (1963). *Prejudice and Your Child.* New York: Bean Press.

Davis, A. Y. (1983). *Women, Race, and Class.* New York: Vintage Books.

Giddings, P. (1984). *When and Where I Enter: The Impact of Black Women on Race and Sex in America.* Toronto: Bantam Books.

Glazer, N., and Moynihan, D. P. (1975). *Ethnicity Theory and Experience.* Cambridge, MA: Harvard University Press.

Griggs, L. B., and Louw, L. L. (1994). *Valuing Diversity.* New York: McGraw-Hill, Inc.

Hacker, A. (1996) "Racial Discrimination Limits Opportunities for Black," in D. Bender and B. Leone (Eds.), *Race Relations: Opposing Viewpoints.* (pp. 74–82), San Diego, CA: Greenhaven Press, Inc.

Henderson, G. (1994). *Cultural Diversity in the Workplace: Issues and Strategies.* Quorum Books.

Jameison, D., and O'Mara, J. (1991). *Managing Workforce 2000: Gaining the Diversity Advantage.* San Francisco, Oxford: Jossey-Bass Publishers.

Jones, E. W. Jr. (May/June, 1986). Black Managers the Dream Deferred. *Harvard Business Review,* (pp. 84–93).

Kuran, T. (1996). "A Backlash Against Affirmative Action Is Growing Among Whites," in D. Bender and B. Leone (Eds.), *Race Relations: Opposing Viewpoints.* (pp. 29–36), San Diego, CA: Greenhaven Press, Inc.

Lerner, G. (1973). *Black Women in White America: A Documentary History.* New York: Vintage Books.

Lord, R. G., and Alliger, G. M. (1985, January). "A Comparison of Four Information Processing Models of Leadership and Social Perceptions," *Human Relations,* Thirty-eight, (1), (pp. 47–65).

Marques, J. M., Robalo, E. M., and Rocha, S. A. (1992, July–August). "In-group Bias and the "Black Sheep" Effect: Assessing the Impact of Social Identification and Perceived Variability on Group Judgments," *European Journal of Social Psychology,* (4) Twenty- two, (pp. 331–352).

Marques, J. M., and Yzerbyt, V. Y. (1988, July). "The Black Sheep Effect: Judgmental Extremity Towards In-Group Members in Inter-and Intra-Group Situations," *European Journal of Social Psychology,* Eighteen, (3), (pp. 287–292).

McIntosh, P. (1988). White Privilege and Male Privilege: A Personal Account of Coming to See Correspondences through Work in Women's Studies. MA: Wellesley College.

Phinney, J. (1990). "Ethnic Identity in Adolescents and Adults: A Review of Research," *Psychological Bulletin,* 108, (pp. 499–514).

Phinney, J. (1992). "The Multigroup Ethnic Identity Measure: A New Scale for Use with Adolescents and Young Adults from Diverse Groups," *Journal of Adolescent Research,* Seven, (pp. 156–176).

Phinney, J. (1989). "Stages of Ethnic Identity Development in Minority Group Adolescents," *Journal of Early Adolescence,* Nine, (pp. 34–49).

Phinney, J. (1993). "A Three-stage Model of Ethnic Identity Development," in M. Bernal and G. Knight (Eds.), *Ethnic Identity: Formation and Transmission Among Hispanics and Other Minorities.* (pp. 61–79). Albany State University of New York Press.

Rothbart, M. Dawes, R., and Park B. (1984). "Stereotyping and Sampling Biases in Intergroup Perception," in R. Eiser (Ed.), *Attitudinal Judgment.* (pp. 109–134).

Rotheram, M. J., and Phinney, J. S. (1987). *Children's Ethnic Socialization: Pluralism and Development.* Sage Publications, Inc.

Sekaran, U., and Leong, F. T. (1992). *Women Power: Managing in Times of Demographic Turbulence.* Sage Publications.

Steele, S. (1990). "I'm Black, You're White, Who's Innocent," in *The Content of Our Character.* New York: St. Martin Press (pp. 1–20).

Tajfel, H. (1982). "Social Psychology of Intergroup Relations," *Annual Review of Psychology,* Thirty-three, (pp. 1–39).

Thomas, R. R., Jr. (1991). *Beyond Race and Gender.* American Management Association.

Thomas, R. R., Jr. (1996). *Redefining Diversity.* American Management Association.

West, C. (1993). *Race Matters.* New York: Vintage Books.

Wilkins, R. (1996). "Affirmative Action Is Still Necessary to Fight Discrimination," in D. Bender and B. Leone (Eds.), *Race Relations: Opposing Viewpoints.* (pp. 102–110), San Diego, CA: Greenhaven Press, Inc.

Williams, J. E., and Morland, J. K. (1976). *Race, Color, and the Young Child.* Chapel Hill: The University of North Carolina Press.

Wilson, W. J. (1973). *Power, Racism, and Privilege.* New York, NY: The Macmillan Company.

Yamato, G. (1992). "Something About the Subject Makes It Hard to Name," in M. L. Anderson and P. H. Collins, *Race, Class, and Gender.* (pp. 66–68). Cambridge, MA: Cambridge University Press.